Signage
Design

Signage

Michelle Galindo

Design

CONTENTS

Creating legible environments
by Michelle Galindo

Wayfinding and signage support the orientation and navigation in architectural structures. Wayfinding encompasses all of the ways in which people orient themselves in physical space and navigate from place to place. It is an aspect of the built environment that spans both the architectural and the graphical realms. Signage visually displays information, with the use of typography and graphics, to help us to understand architecture and infrastructure, and communicate about the identity of a structure. Both, wayfinding and signage are integral elements for structures.

This book includes a large number of international examples in different typologies, where design, communication and identity come together to help us experience spaces and places in enriched ways – through wayfinding and signage. The directional and environmental graphics by Latitude Group applied to the

QV Parking Garage Wayfinding design is a two-dimensional, eye-catching, large-scale, hand painted typography sign with overlaying colors. Other designs, such as Quinta das Flores Secondary School by R2, translates an idea in a minimalistic way to guide the users throughout the space; the school's relationship to music was the beginning point for their design, in which the sound intensity was translated on the typeface by differentiating the density according to the numerical value of the level. While other designs aim to transmit a message; Morisawa Corporate Headquarter Building, a font maker company by Hiromura Design Office, uses three-dimensional forms and shadows of the typography signs to convey the importance and existence of the typography role in our society.

Signage and wayfinding design are not an easy task, considerations such as spatial complexity and sight lines to destinations

from different locations throughout the site are important. The users and visitors depend on systems of visual, audible, and tactile cues not only to lead the way, but also to keep them safe. Whether in a museum, hospital, airport, mall, or street in an unfamiliar city, navigation, directional information, orientation or interpretation must be supported in an effective way. An in- depth case study of the visual environment, stream of users, detailed prints of the building and other factors should be integrated into the design.

For instance, traffic navigation wayfinding design, is not simply about applying some eye-catching graphics. Multi-story parking garages have a complex set of navigation challenges that the wayfinding information designer has to address. The needs of both pedestrian and motorist differentiate between arrival and departure journeys. They also need to take account of the competing distractions vying for driver's attention – the hunt for vacant spaces, looking out for reversing cars and avoiding distracted pedestrians. All in an environment where line of sight can be obscured by parked cars, walls, columns and pedestrians shoppers.

//

The wayfinding and signage designs presented in this volume have an important role in encompassing both the experience of choosing a path within a built environment and the set of design elements that aid in such a decision. The successful designs integrate society by blurring the lines between the different cultures, languages and ages, meet the demands of the times by creating user-friendly signs, effective use of graphics, colors and shapes and creative, tailor-made pictograms to guide the everyday users of a building and/or space and explore signage as a point where architecture and graphic design collide. The book showcases great examples of signage design worldwide, ranging from museums and schools to traffic navigation systems, with an emphasis on the most original approaches to leading the way.

//

Balancing style and functionality with the visibility, readability constraints and the ease of use of the wayfinding in the built environment causes an effect on the way we work, relax, travel and interact. The one hundred-plus projects presented in this volume feature diverse aspects of the discipline. *Signage Design* offers a view into some of the work of some of the world's most prominent design firms and sign experts in this rapidly evolving discipline.

מעבדת עיצוב

Design Lab

مختبر تصميم

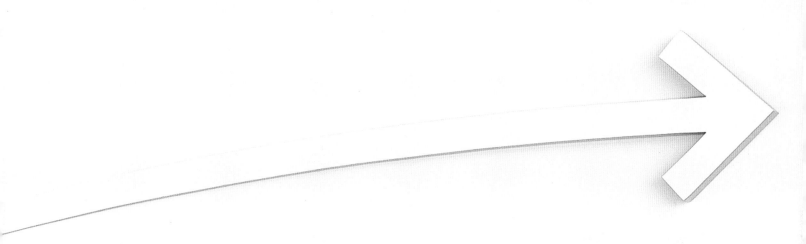

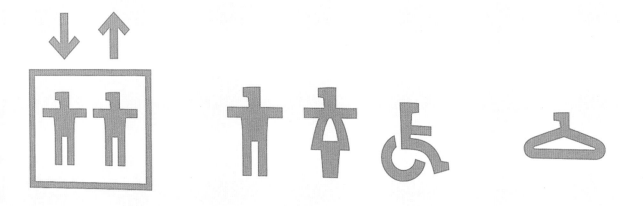

CULTURE

Adi Stern Design

מעבדת עיצוב
Design Lab
مختبر تصميم

↑↑ | **Informational signs**
↖ | **Trilingual entrance sign** in Hebrew, Arabic and Latin
↑ | **Detail arrow**

Design Museum Holon
Holon

The museum's signage and wayfinding system challenges traditional approaches, using white arrows, designed by Atelier, Doron Rokach on white walls. Primarily discernible from the shadows they cast, the arrows emerge from the walls and transform from two- to three-dimensional forms. The shape of the arrows echoes the flow and movement of the Corten weathering steel bands surrounding the building. The challenge was to create a signage system that is visible and easy to use, while not competing with Arad's dynamic architecture. The system is trilingual, using Hebrew, Arabic, and Latin. It also includes a custom Hebrew typeface designed specifically for the project.

PROJECT FACTS

Address: Pinhas Eilon St. 8, Holon 58459, Israel. **Client:** Municipality of Holon. **Completion:** 2010.
Architect: Ron Arad. **Typeface:** Custom Hebrew. **Function:** Museum.

↑ | **Two- to three-dimensional arrows**
↓ | **Arrow indicating the direction** of the
upper gallery

↑ | **White directional arrow**
↓ | **Pictograms and typography**

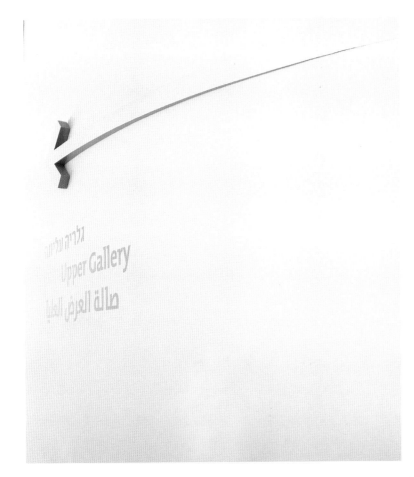

מוזיאון העיצוב חולון
Design Museum Holon
متحف التّصميم حولون

↑ | **Informational signage** on embossed, spaced and coated metal plates

OK Center for Contemporary Art
Linz

The interior and exterior wayfinding systems were developed for a new cultural hub consisting of two exhibition halls, restaurants, offices and a large square in the historical center of Linz. It was necessary to take the existing historical buildings, contemporary architecture and the surrounding urban space into account. The system, using embossed, spaced and coated metal plates, reacts to all backgrounds and surfaces. White and gray are used in-house, while steel and black are used on the square.

Address: OK-Platz 1, 4020 Linz, Austria. **Client:** OK Center for Contemporary Art. **Completion:** 2007.
Function: Exhibition, restaurant and offices.

↑ | Interior floor level sign
↓ | Font pictographs

↑ | Steel signs

abcdefghijklmnopqrstuvwxyz

ABCDEFGHIJKLM NOPQRSTUVWXYZ

1234567890

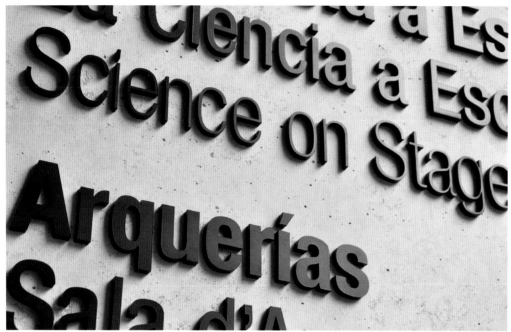

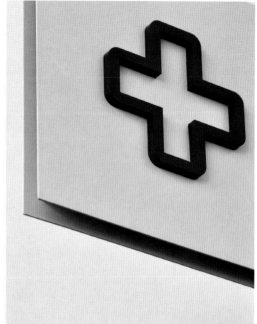

↖↖ | **Wall sign** with sharp sans serif
typography in bold and light styles
↑↑ | **Service sign**
↖ | **Informative wall sign at parking entry**
↑ | **Lobby sign (vestíbulo)**

City of the Arts and Sciences
Valencia

The CAC – Ciudad de las Artes y las Ciencias (City of Arts and Sciences) signage system
is an example of how to elaborate a concept that harmonizes with the surrounding architecture. Fitting into a Santiago Calatrava project is no easy task as forms are bold and the
palette is usually minimal. Competing forms should be prevented but at the same time they
must be noticeable, as visitors must locate these effortlessly while navigating the park.
BOSCO accomplished a bold, rich yet simple solution to accompany the surrounding context and lead visitors around the CAC. Sharp sans serif typography in bold and light styles
contrasts from its applied material (white panel, fabric, perforated metal or concrete). Simple mono icons developed for the project are easy to notice and clear to follow.

Address: Avenida Autopista del Saler, nº 3, 46013 Valencia, Spain. **Client:** Ciudad de las Artes y las Ciencias. **Completion:** 2010. **Digital signage system:** ToDo. **Typeface:** Sherif Sans. **Function:** Museum.

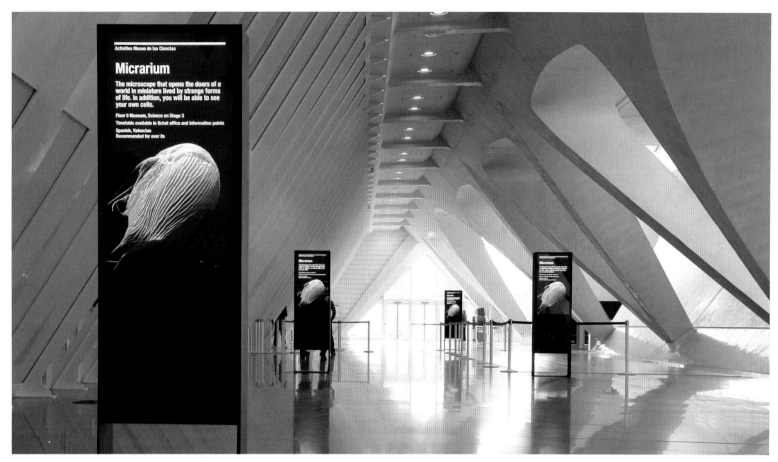

↑ | **Informative and directional digital signs**
↓ | **Ticket desks' digital signs**

↓ | **Informative digital sign**

↑ | External entry signage

Australian Center for the Moving Image
Melbourne

This wayfinding project focused on the pedestrian and transportation behavior happenning around Federation Square. The concept for the signage came from the idea that ACMI, greater than the sum of its parts, forms the white light created by the visible spectrum of moving images. The dramatic angles and shards of colored light suggest movement and transformation, even in stationary signage, as visitors move around their three-dimensional forms. Central to the signage are the major monolithic sign at the pedestrian entry on FED Square and the large illuminated letterforms on Flinders Street.

PROJECT FACTS

Address: Federation Square, Flinders Street, Melbourne VIC 3000, Australia. **Client:** Australian Center for the Moving Image. **Completion:** 2009. **Completion:** Soren Luckins, Fin Bluter, Nick LeMeussurier. **Function:** Cultural institution.

↑ | Level directory
↓ | Monolithic sign at the pedestrian entry

↑ | Monolithic sign

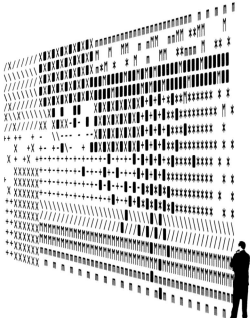

↖↖ | Perforated informational wall
↑↑ | View from the rear rooms accross the foyer
↖ | Signage system applied to the walls and floor
↑ | ASCII pattern

SKIN – Pavilion of Knowledge
Lisbon

This environmental design project consists of a multipurpose room, the foyer of the Pavilion of Knowledge and the Science Museum in Lisbon. The intention, due to the versatility of the usage of this space, was to create a texture with the use of a perforated wall with acoustic and lighting purposes. The theme, ASCII (American Standard Code for Information Interchange) is an analogy to museums' intents' of sharing information. This idea was achieved by creating different pattern densities with bigger or smaller cuts, acoustic percentages and the openings in the window areas of the rear rooms. LED white lighting between the wall and the SKIN was balanced with natural light.

PROJECT FACTS

Location: Lisbon, Portugal. **Client:** Pavilion of Knowledge (Ciência Viva). **Completion:** 2010. **Architect:** JLCG Architects. **Manufacturer:** ACF (Arlindo Correia & Filhos) Demetro a Metro. **Function:** Museum.

↑ | Perforated wall texture
↓ | Plates scheme + acoustic scheme

↑ | LED lighting between the wall and the SKIN

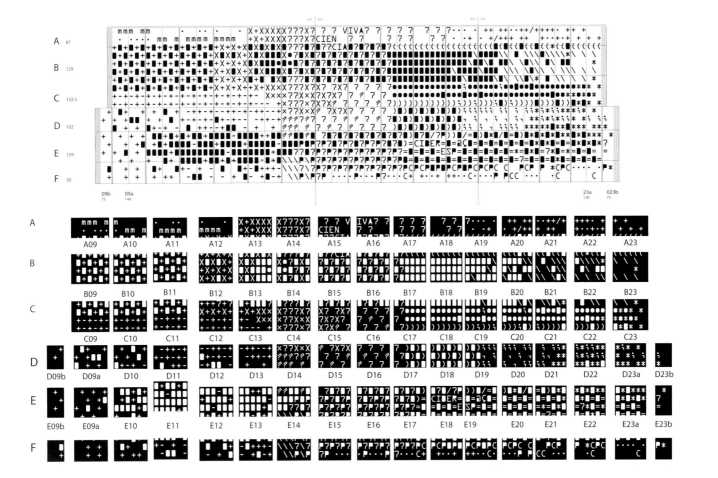

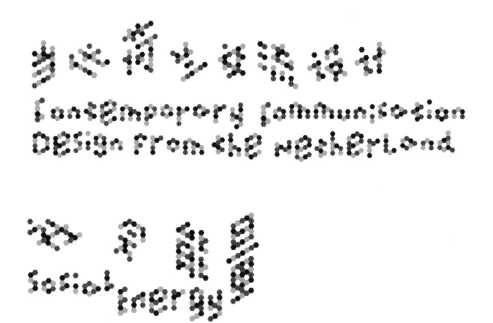

↖↖ | **Typography**
↑↑ | **Façade sign** with large red, white and blue light elements
↖ | **Façade sign** with large red, white and blue light elements
↑ | **Billboard** with hexagonal single molecules form the sign

Social Energy
Shenzhen

"Social Energy" is an exhibition which comprehensively presents Dutch communication design in China. The exhibition strives for leading the charge. It took place in the first Chinese museum for vanguard design. Therefore, different places were illuminated following the architecture of the art museum. Hexagonal single molecules are put together to form large red, white and blue light elements. By means of inflatable devices, the installation can also be employed on water surfaces.

PROJECT FACTS
Location: Shenzhen, China. **Client:** The OCT Art & Design Gallery, Shenzhen. **Completion:** 2009. **Graphic design and typographers:** Hei Yiyang, Liu Zhao, Wang Xiaomeng. **Function:** Exhibition.

↑↑ | Entrance floor with walk-in map, animated by arrows
↑ | 28 panel showcasing individual stories
↗ | Cinema featuring the stories of the witnesses

"You and Us"
Stuttgart

The history of people who have been displaced is told through the concerted use of different kinds of media. A walkable map of the banishment areas depicts the origins of displaced persons through hundreds of animated arrows marking the routes of their escape. A curved wall guides visitors towards an enormous, slowly rotating "banishment" door, leading into the main room of the exhibition, the Field of Encounter. Here, 28 veterans are telling 28 authentic stories. Mirrored walls extend the field of the veterans infinitely in all directions.

PROJECT FACTS
Location: Stuttgart, Germany. **Client:** Haus der Geschichte Baden-Württemberg.
Completion: 2009. **Graphic designer:** Daniel Naegele, Anina Stocker, Gerd Häußler.
Function: Exhibition.

↑ | Façade with mono colored graphics

Go with God (Vai com Deus)
Porto

R2 Design's application of graphics to this centuries old building is visual and tactile. It takes the art of relief to a new level of communication. This display of text shows the impact that mono colored graphics have, and the interest they create without bombarding the senses in this ancient corridor. The graphics speak of the building's past. Just as the promises of God were spoken for countless centuries on the inside of this old church, now they exist on the outside of the same walls. The building is now a gallery for local artists.

PROJECT FACTS

Location: Porto, Portugal. **Client:** Dr. Eduardo Fernandes, Ermida Nossa Senhora da Conceição, Belém. **Completion:** 2009. **Typeface:** Knockout. **Function:** Gallery.

↑ | The graphics speak of the building's past
↓ | Visual and tactile graphics

↑ | Knockout typeface
↓ | Promises of God written on the façade

↖ | **Exhibition signage** made of light
↑↑ | **Exhibition** light sign on floor surface
↑ | **Informational sign** on metal plate

Creative Lab Signed by Tenente
Lisbon

"Creative laboratory" was the starting point for the dialogue and interaction between all disciplines involved in the space; the exhibition was intended to be a conceptual continuity of the aesthetics of the fashion designer JAT. A long piece of black fabric, alternates between linear walls and curved pleats, opaque and translucent elements in basic bare scenery. Mirrored lettering under the black veil and lettering made of light avoid all physical elements besides the minimal scenery created. Extra care in the balance between natural and artificial lighting, reinforce the entire scenic environment.

Location: Lisbon, Portugal. **Client:** MUDE – Museum of Design and Fashion of Lisbon. **Completion:** 2010. **Architect:** SAMI Architects. **Function:** Exhibition.

↑ | **Exhibition platform** display with signate on the surface
↓ | **Exhibition signage** made out of light displayed on the floor

↑ | **Informational signage** on exhibition platform

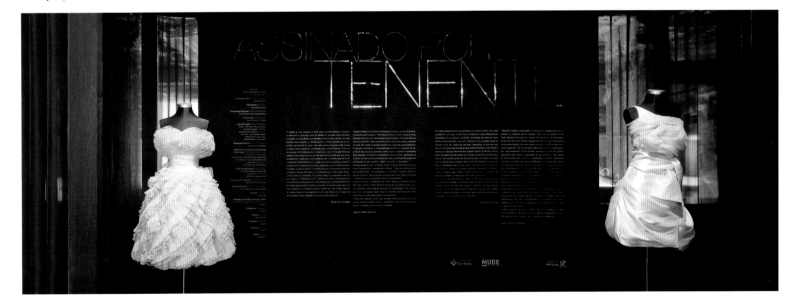

L2M3 Kommunikation
design

↖ | Glass surface with informational
signage
↑↑ | Identificational sign at entrance
↑ | Informational signage

Ruhr Museum
Essen

One part of the Zollverein Coal Mine world cultural heritage site is the former coal wash plant, converted by Rem Kohlhaas that has housed the Ruhr Museum since January 2010. Visitors experience a succession of very different impressions and discover an equally chequered history. The visual identity in the form of DNA code is constituted by a typographical system that imprints itself in different aggregate states into the exhibition. Based on the idea of a mine car or container, the individual words sit more or less exactly in a grid system of areas. This gives rise to a rhythm that appears mechanical and which is formulated in the form of graphics and objects.

PROJECT FACTS

Address: Gelsenkirchener Straße 181, 45309 Essen, Germany. **Client:** Stiftung Zollverein, Essen.
Completion: 2010. **Architect interior exhibition:** hg merz architekten museumsgestalter. **Function:** Museum.

↑ | Informational signage in main exhibition space
↓ | Overhead lit signage

↑ | Typographical system integrated into the exhibition
↓ | Detail informational signage

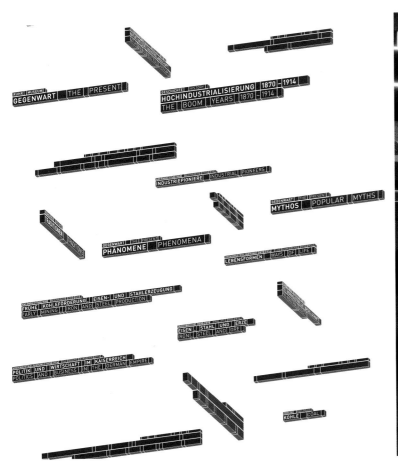

MAXXI National Museum of XXI Century Art
Rome

↖↖ | **Museum entrance** with tailor-made freestanding sign
↑↑ | **Three-dimensional directional signage**, gallery 2
↖ | **MAXXI logo** painted on the perimeter gates
↑ | **Three-dimensional directional signage**, gallery 5

Ma:design conceived the signage system of MAXXI to reflect the architectural concepts of using light and shadow, full and empty, and rigid and organic shapes. An over scaled version of the MAXXI logo painted on the perimeter gates in black and white identifies the exterior, without touching the cement skin. The building's perimeter windows, marked for security reasons, act as communicative surfaces, decorated with aphorisms and quotes from modern art and architecture. Inside the hall, a large, full-color, indoor LED display follows the curved contours of the wall and provides real-time information, images, and suggestions relevant to the current exhibitions, meetings, and initiatives scheduled in the museum.

PROJECT FACTS

Address: Via Guido Reni, 4 A 00196 Rome, Italy. **Client:** Fondazione MAXXI. **Completion:** 2010. **Architect:** Zaha Hadid Architects. **Manufacturer:** Arpa pubblicità srl (wayfinding structures, videowall), G2 (gate painting). **Function:** Museum.

↑ | **Perimeter windows** decorated with quotes from art and architecture
↓ | **Letters in exhibition room** seem to spring from the wall

↓ | **Three-dimensional directional signage,** third floor

← | **Three-dimensional gallery** room number
↙ | **Exhibition room denomination**
↓ | **Elevator information signage**

← | Gallery 1: three-dimensional number and map
↙ | Informational signage
↓ | Three-dimensional coat room and restroom sign

Mary Choueiter

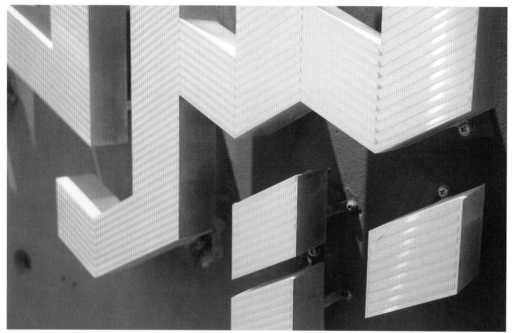

↑↑ | **Main sign in Arabic**
↖ | **Detail of the sign pattern treatment**
↑ | **Preliminary studies and sketches for Latin and Arabic type treatment**

Beirut Exhibition Center
Beirut

Beirut's exhibition center received a visual identity where East meets West. The inspiration for the identity came from the building which distorts the surrounding environment though its corrugated reflective mirror façade, designed by L.E.F.T Architects. Lebanese-born, Brooklyn-based Mary Choueiter distorted both the Arabic and Latin alphabets to capture the architectures vision. This project is the visual identity of the Beirut Exhibition Center; a non-profit space that provides a collaborative environment for art museums, galleries, artist collectives and cultural institutions. The corporate identity applications included the primary and secondary bilingual signage in Arabic and Latin through custom typography design.

Location: Beirut, Lebanon. **Completion:** 2010. **Architects:** L.E.F.T Architects. **Typeface:** Arabic and Latin custom typography. **Typeface:** Arabic and Latin custom typography. **Function:** Art Gallery.

↑ | **Detail typography**
↓ | **Bilingual (Arabic and English) street sign**

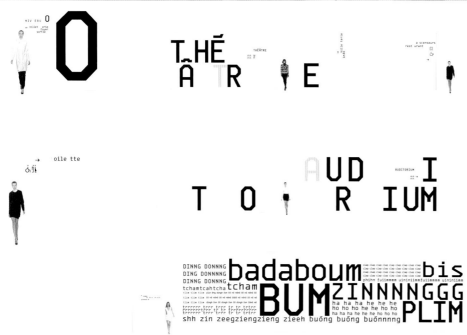

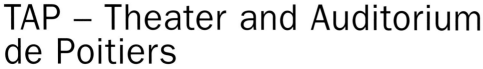

↑↑ | **Parking signage**
↖ | **Elevation schemes** of the applied lettering
↑ | **Parking spots** reserved for handicapped

TAP – Theater and Auditorium de Poitiers
Poitiers

The design approach started simultaneously with the wayfinding system and the chromatic study of the building. The concept for the wayfinding system was inspired from the Dada movement. Words and letters are freely arranged and partially expressed in an onomatopoeic way. The building is literally a container for words and sounds. The guidance system consists of oversized letters and numerals recognizable from a wider distance. To announce the events of each season, guidelines were developed for the exterior video projections in the glass "skin" of the building, like a deconstructed video screen with moving images. An exterior signage system consisting of "totems" in the surroundings of the building is the limit of the design project.

Address: 1 Place Mar Leclerc, 86000 Poitiers, France. **Completion:** 2008. **Architect:** João Luís Carrilho da Graça/ jlcg architects. **Signage and graphics fabrication design:** Demetro a Metro. **Function:** Theater and auditorium.

↑ | **Words and letters** freely arranged on wall and ceiling
↓ | **Signage in auditorium area**

↑ | **Exterior informational signage**

↖ | **Tale rendered** on the ceiling
↑ | **Concrete panel** with styrofoam letters
placed in a formwork

House of Tales
(Casa do Conto)
Porto

Rather than trying to restore or recreate the original artwork of this 19th century cultural treasure, the architects instead found an unexpected way to project the same content and subject matter through the use of typography, in turn creating an eerie and haunting installation. A group of individuals familiar with the space, who had been involved with its restoration process before the fire, were asked to write about each of the spaces – the tales were rendered on the ceilings into concrete panels using Styrofoam letters placed in a formwork. Each text was assigned a different graphic style, allowing the subject matter and tone to guide their graphic interpretation.

PROJECT FACTS

Location: Porto, Portugal. **Client:** Casa do Conto (House of Tales) Arts & Residence. **Completion:** 2011.
Typeface: Ordinaire, Neutrafaceslab, Jannon, Dada and Futura. **Manufacturer:** Pedras de Ronfos Lda.
Function: Exhibition.

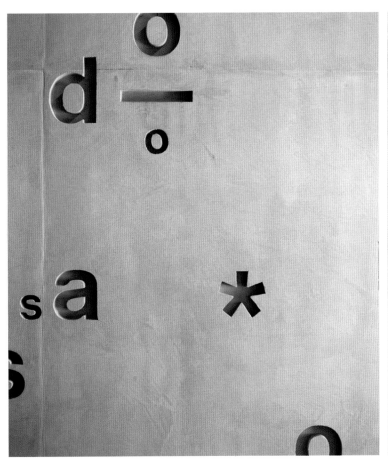

↑ | **Legible type size and depth**
↓ | **Ceiling motifs**

↑ | **Phrase** set into concrete panel using
styrofoam letters

↑ | **Exhibition space** with view to cardboard box installation
→ | **Nine-meter high cardboard cube display**

Building for the 2000-Watt Society: The State of Affairs
Zurich

Commissioned by the City of Zurich and hosted by the Selnau transformer substation, the "Energy Mountain" exemplifies "sustainable building" as a key ecological issue. It consists of a nine-meter high installation of 500 cardboard cubes that display pioneering accomplishments of Swiss architecture. The architecture examples are split into six groups, each themed with a color and with theoretical text written on the cardboard cubes, printed in black and white in Interstate typography. Every possible weight on the font from extra thin to super bold, is used to adjust the various reading situations on the cardboard box installation.

Location: Zurich, Switzerland. **Client:** City of Zurich. **Completion:** 2009. **Architect:** Holzer Kobler. **Typeface:** Interstate. **Function:** Exhibition.

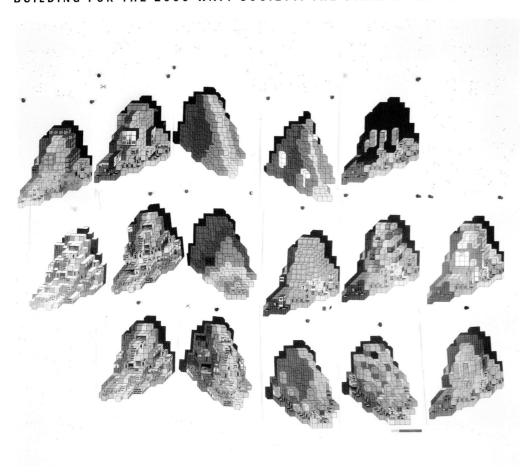

←← | **Cardboard cubes** displaying information
← | **Diagrammatic sketches**
↓ | **Detailed project information** is displayed at eye level

↑ | Donors' wall

Hoffmann Building Signs for Aldeburgh Music
Snape, Suffolk

Aldeburgh Music opened a new campus in a former malting building last year. Architect Haworth Tompkins kept the industrial feel, retaining many exposed surfaces, to reflect the building's heritage. Silk Pearce's design of the signs and environmental graphics is similarly sensitive to the location. Working from detailed design layouts, a traditional sign writer painted directly onto the walls and doors. The carefully chosen colors reflect the architect's color scheme, while the uppercase San Serif typeface strikes a balance between Victorian sign writing and a contemporary design approach.

PROJECT FACTS **Address:** Snape, Suffolk, England, United Kingdom. **Client:** Aldeburgh Music. **Completion:** 2009. **Architect:** Haworth Tompkins Architects. **Typographers:** Peter Silk and Rob Steer. **Signwriter:** Simon Clark. **Function:** Music school.

↑ | Britten Studio directional signage
↓ | Jerwood Kiln Studio engraved signage
at door

↑ | Britten Studio balcony door with
signage on door frame

Studio FM Milano

↖↖ | **Display information hanging from ceiling**
↑↑ | **White arrow indicating exhibition direction**
↖ | **Three-dimensional exhibition sign**
↑ | **Informational signage on wall**

Triennale Design Museum
Milan

The hypothesis behind this interpretation of the Design Museum focuses on the close relationship between the processes of invention and production; the exhibition narrates the stories of these objects, whose history is precisely the criterion behind their presence and position in the exhibition scenario. The tables displayed groupings of objects at a comfortable height for viewing, but also functioned like the tables of a workshop, on which objects are placed to catch the attention of the visitor. The graphics were both carved in the bended backlit corian walls, and serigraphed on the surface.

PROJECT FACTS

Location: Milan, Italy. **Client:** Triennale Design Museum. **Completion:** 2009. **Architect:** Antonio Citterio, Patricia Viel and Partners. **Function:** Museum.

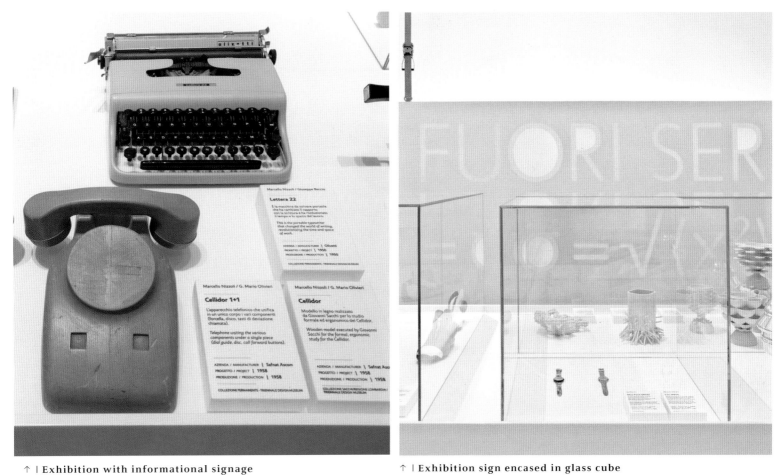

↑ | Exhibition with informational signage on table display
↓ | Exhibition information display

↑ | Exhibition sign encased in glass cube

↑ | **Exterior signage**

Kalmar Art Museum
Kalmar

The Kalmar Art Museum (Kalmar Konstmuseum) is a new space for contemporary art in southern Sweden. Sweden Graphics designed a new typeface called Kalmar Sans which is available to the museum in a stencil and a non-stencil version – the stencil for big type and the other for smaller type in print. By masking out big squares on the wall and placing the type mask, the designers created a signage system that helps the users find their way around the museum. The base for the sign is a yellow square which is also the base for the logo and graphics that appear in the stationary. This square is painted directly over the concrete surface, and at some locations it passes over surfaces in laquered wood and accentuates the idea that the square is sort of "slapped on". The slate logo (3 x 3 meters) is solid concrete and it is stuck it into the soil outside the museum.

PROJECT FACTS

Address: Stadsparken, 392 33 Kalmar, Sweden. **Completion:** 2008. **Architect:** Tham & Videgård Arkitekter. **Typeface:** Kalmar Sans. **Function:** Museum of contemporary art.

↑ | Informational sign
↓ | First floor foyer with informational signage painted on walls

↑ | Second floor gallery signage

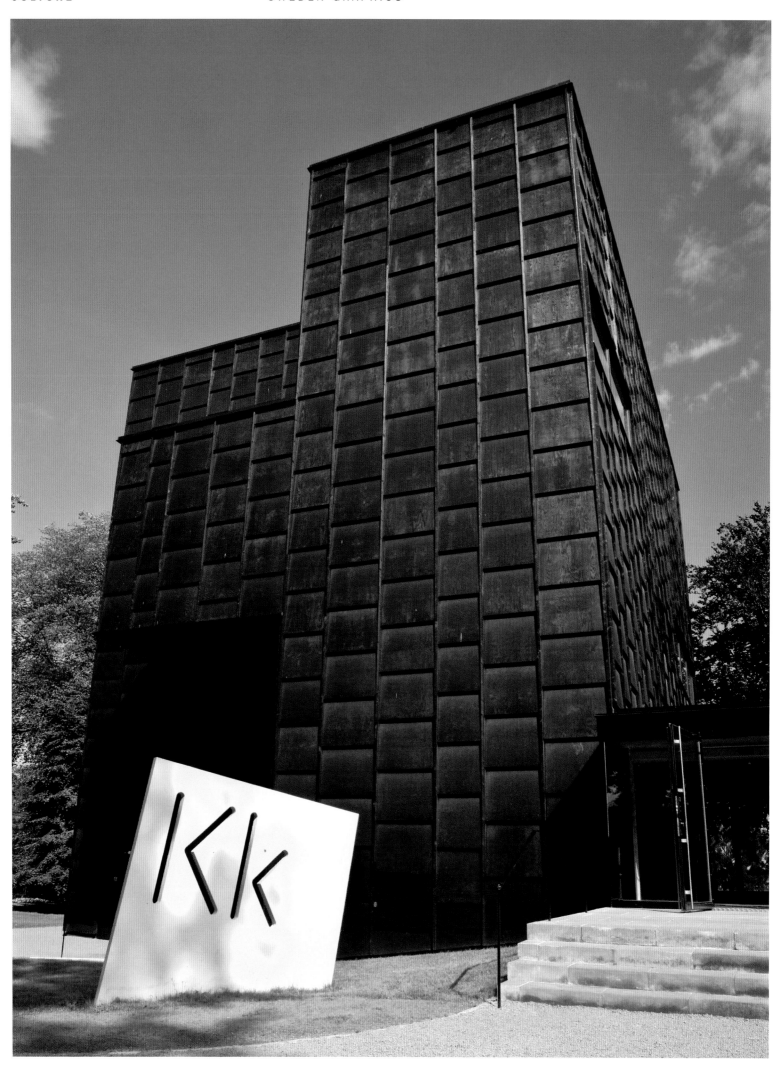

← ← | **Exterior sign**
← | **Fourth floor gallery signage**
↓ | **Custom typeface**

Kalmar sans stencil
ABCDEFGHIJKLMNOPQRSTUVXYZÅÄÖ
abcdefghijklmnopqrstuvxyzåäö
0123456789

Kalmar sans
ABCDEFGHIJKLMNOPQRSTUVXYZÅÄÖ
abcdefghijklmnopqrstuvxyzåäö
0123456789

Gruppe Gut

THE ALPS   A WORK OF ART

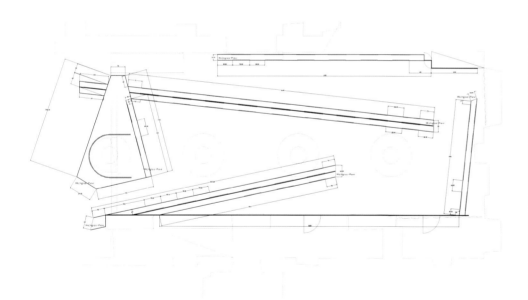

↖↖ | **Identification sign at entrance**
↑↑ | **White block** which acts as an informational sign
↖ | **Floor plan shows room assignment**
↑ | **Informational signage**

The Alps – A Work of Art
Bolzano

The Alps – A work of Art holds an exhibition about geological photos of Bernhard Edmaier. The idea was to interpret the various "form changings", a mountain goes through, as the viewer changes his and her point of view. At the entrance the same idea is applied with a typographical anamorphosis. In the exhibition, the photographs are displayed in passe-partouts, so there is always just one picture fully visible – just by "hiking through", the user will discover new pictures, like new point of views. Furthermore the design is an interpretation of the geological alpine formations of the Dolomites, with their straight white rocks.

PROJECT FACTS   **Location:** Bolzano, Italy. **Client:** Museum of Nature South Tyrol. **Completion:** 2011. **Function:** Museum / exhibition.

53

↑ | Sign with typographical anamorphosis
↓ | Exhibition signage

Frost* Design

↖↖ | Directional color-coded signage
↖ | Monolithic block signage wrapped around column
↑ | Bold color-coding numbers on central column

Powerhouse Museum
Sydney

Frost* Design designed a new internal wayfinding system, integrating identification and directional signage to facilities, temporary exhibits, and the museum's permanent collection. To reference the building's industrial history and to capture the essence of a modern design museum, a family of bold, dynamic signs, distinct from the exhibition signage system was used. The five-story building has various entry points for different visitor groups, making navigation a major issue. By masterplanning typical visitor journeys, the designers were able to identify and position new signage in appropriate locations for specific audiences. To work with the detailed interior color scheme, signs were designed with large white fields as a canvas to hold wayfinding information and simple white monolithic blocks were color-coded to the floor level.

PROJECT FACTS   **Location:** Sydney, Australia. **Client:** Powerhouse Museum. **Completion:** 2007. **Function:** Museum.

55

↑ | **Level two informational signage with map**
↓ | **Monumental numbers at the top of the escalators**

↑ | **Industrial looking signage**

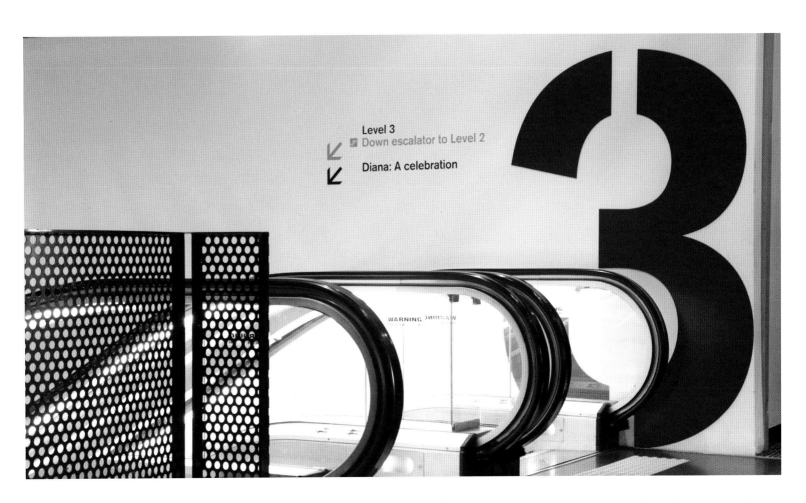

Erik Schmitt and Julio
Martinez/ Studio1500

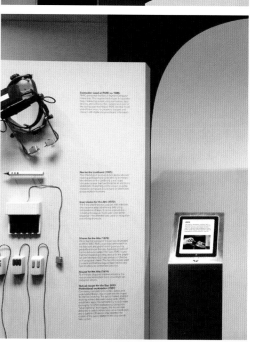

↖↖ | **Ethnography display** in foreground
↑↑ | **Ipad stand**
↖ | **Exterior view** through secondary
entrance
↑ | **Exhibition signage** of small devices and
ipad stand

Room 2306 PARC
Innovation Exhibit
Palo Alto (CA)

An exhibit was designed for PARC, the legendary center for technology innovation and R&D
in Silicon Valley. Many of PARC's key breakthrough innovations – including the Laser Print-
er, the personal computing workstation (including the mouse, icons, and "windows"), and the
development of Ethernet – needed to be showcased within the space. However, it was also
essential that the research center's current endeavors be highlighted as well. To achieve this
balance of showcasing the past and the future, historic artifacts were placed on top of clean,
contemporary platforms, while bold graphics, videos, and interactive ipad presentations on
custom designed stands detailed the ongoing innovation taking place at PARC.

Location: Palo Alto (CA), USA. **Client:** PARC, a Xerox Company. **Completion:** 2011. **Function:** Center for technology innovation and R&D.

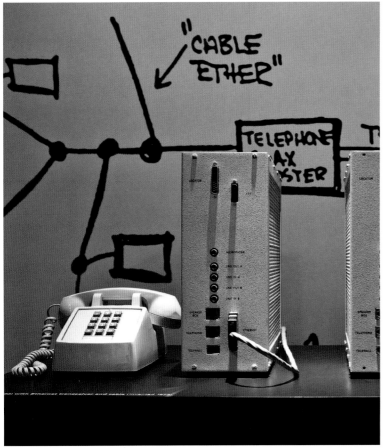

↑ | **Informational signage** of ethernet artifacts
↓ | **View through main entrance**

↑ | **Exhibition informational sign**
↓↓ | **East elevation design study**

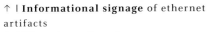

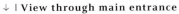

↖↖ | **Identificational signage** in two languages
↖ | **Informational exhibition design**
↑ | **Informational signage**

Shanghai World Expo, 2010
Shangai

Troika has been commissioned by the Foreign and Commonwealth Office to create three new art installations for UK's Pavilion at the Shanghai 2010 World Expo to be displayed alongside the main UK pavilion. Instead of a classical exhibition design, Troika devised a narrative concept consisting of three immersive and multi-layered installations inviting the visitors to experience the pavilion through all their senses. In each walkway leading to and away from the Seed Cathedral unfolds an installation, part of a triptyque narrative presenting the relationship between Nature and the British cities, past, present and future.

PROJECT FACTS Location: Shanghai, China. **Client:** Foreign & Commonwealth Office. **Completion:** 2010. **Pavilion architect:** Heatherwick Studio. **Function:** Exhibition, installations for the UK Pavilion.

↑ | **Informational signage** in two languages
↓ | **Pavilion exhibition**

↓ | **View to pavilion exhibition**

Günter Hermann
Architekten

↑↑ | **Large scale signage painted on concrete wall**
↖ | **Bathroom painted sign**
↑ | **Ramp**

Cinema Wöhrden West
Tuttlingen

Located in Tuttlingen near the shore of the Danube river, the "Wöhrden West" district was restructured as part of an urban development measure. In addition to a multiplex cinema with 833 seats in five theaters and dining facilities, three further buildings were created. The current urban planning concept of the Wöhrdenkopf is dominated by the cinema and administration hub. The cinema building design is based on light and shadow as an art form. The theaters are visibly stacked on top of each other and accessible via stairs and ramps from the Danube side. The exterior cover consists of glass façades with a suspended metal mesh that presents clear vision to the outside and the inside.

PROJECT FACTS
Address: In Wöhrden, 78532 Tuttlingen, Germany. **Client:** Tuttlinger Wohnbau. **Completion:** 2004. **Function:** Cinema.

↑↑ | **Large scale room number
supergraphics**
↑ | **Room number supergraphics from
floor-to-ceiling**
↗ | **Exterior identity sign with lighting
behind**

Cinema Paradiso
St. Pölten

The cinema offers an entry to the world of films, dreams, adventure, and memories. Unlike television, cinema is a place of common adventure. Cinema Paradiso is a place with a unique identity and atmosphere that plays a vital role in the city center with functions that go far beyond merely showing films as an alternative to television. It is a new kind of cinema offering a mixture of catering, film show, repertory cinema and an open center for arts and culture. The versatile division of spaces creates meeting points for communication and entertainment. The transitions between rooms are seamless and open, supported by color and light.

PROJECT FACTS
Address: Rathausplatz 15-S7, 3100 St. Pölten, Austria. **Client:** Verein Cinema Paradiso.
Completion: 2002. **Function:** Cinema, open cultural center and bar.

Erik Schmitt and Julio
Martinez/ Studio1500

↖↖ | **Exhibition supergraphics**
↑↑ | **Exhibit entry identity**
↖ | **Exterior entryway signage**
↑ | **Interior information graphic screens**

Computer History Museum Revolution Exhibit Signage
Mountain View (CA)

The Computer History Museum opened Revolution: a major 25,000 square foot new exhibition. The opening marked a major milestone in the history of the Museum, as it transformed the entire space and presented their vast collection – from the abacus to the smart phone – in a whole new way. A series of materials were designed to support the exhibition, including an identity and signage.

PROJECT FACTS
Location: Mountain View (CA), USA. **Client:** Computer History Museum. **Completion:** 2011. **Function:** Museum.

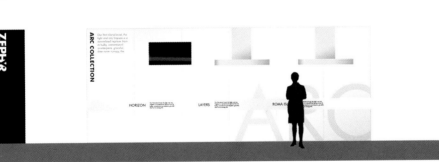
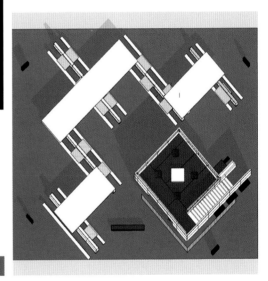

↑↑ | Identification signage
↑ | Main display area and design detail
study
↗↗ | Exhibition design signage
↗ | Floor plan

Zephyr Exhibit
San Francisco (CA)

Zephyr, a manufacturer of designer kitchen hoods, wanted to create a compelling exhibit
environment to launch a new line of products. The 15 x 18 meter space was composed of
staggered walls and overlapping roof panels that gave the space a distinctive contemporary
architectural feeling. The hoods were shown against crisp white walls, with focused lighting and no competing visual elements to emphasize their striking designs.

PROJECT FACTS
Location: San Francisco (CA), USA. **Client:** Zephyr. **Completion:** 2008. **Function:** Exhibition.

↑ | Delegations corridor pavement signage

NATO Summit Lisbon 2010
Lisbon

The scale of the space (35,000 square meters), thousands of users, the complex system of permissions and restrictions in circulation and the costs of an ephemeral two days event were the main constraints in the design of the NATO Summit. Chromatic and aesthetic options were reduced to the essential in order to create a visible, clear, and effective wayfinding system. The black carpet in the main circulation area or "dorsal spine", features white inscriptions. On the center of the main conference hall, an informational image illustrates the pavement.

PROJECT FACTS Location: Lisbon, Portugal. **Completion:** 2010. **Architect:** Risco Architects. **Function:** Summit meetings of Heads of State and Government.

↑ | **Lighting installation and pavement signage**
↓ | **Delegations entrance signage**

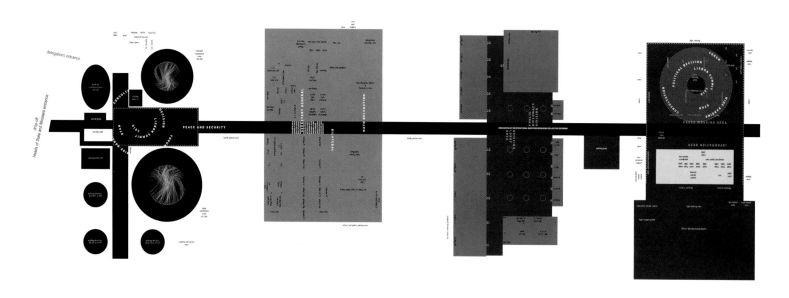

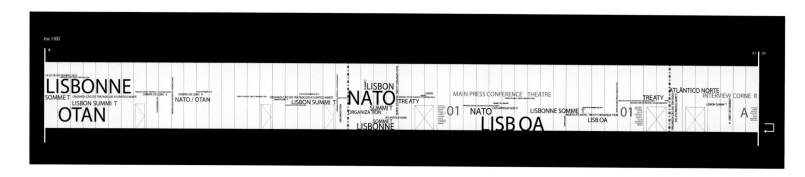

←← | **Large scale restrooms signs** on MDF wall surfaces painted in white
↙↙ | **Floor plans and elevation**
← | **Briefing room with informational signage**
↓ | **Delegations' offices** with signage in three different languages

| Zup Associati Design

↖ | Identiy sign covers concrete platform
↑↑ | Informational signage in pedestrian way
↑ | Guideline map

Shaping the Global Design Agenda International Design Casa
Turin

The external signs installations to the eleven exhibition venues required to perform the dual purpose of signposting the exhibition entrances and indicating the location in relation to the overall route. Benches are used to indicate the entrances dend offer an opportunity to rest and the tables are used for consulting the maps and materials. The flat surfaces of these pieces were employed as directional elements, indicating the routes to take and the distances relative to all of the network destinations. The color green denoted locations that formed part of the Turin World Design Capital circuit. These placemarks portray the exhibition venues while creating a relatively economic temporary urban furnishing system, without neglecting recyclability and sustainability.

Location: Turin, Italy. **Client:** The Torino 2008 World Design Capital Organising Committee. **Completion:** 2008. **Placemarks' manufacturer:** Nord Zinc Company. **Function:** International design conference.

↑ | **Informational "totem"**
↓ | **Color-coded directional signage**

↑ | **Exhibition posters**
↓ | **Color-coded directional signage** painted from wall-to-floor

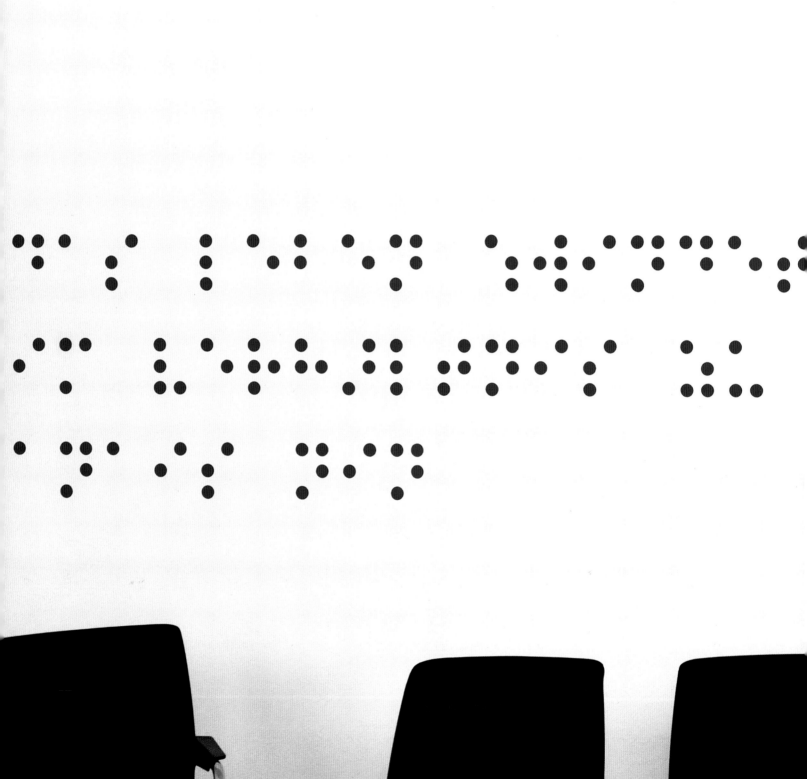

EDUCATION

Abbott Miller/ Pentagram

↖ | **Donor's signage cascades** down the underside of a lobby staircase
↑↑ | **Lettering on the blades** engages multiple surfaces
↑ | **Donor's signage** appears on vertical corner guards outside the classroom doors

The Cooper Union
New York

Abbott Miller and his team at Pentagram designed signage and environmental graphics for the Cooper Union's new academic building, designed by the Pritzker Prize-winning architect Thom Mayne of Morphosis. The program included identification, wayfinding and donor signage and is fully integrated with the building's innovative architecture. The new building canopy features optically extruded lettering that appears "correct" when seen in strict elevation, but distorts as the profile of the letter is dragged backwards in space. An ambitious installation of donor signage is displayed above the stairway that descends through the "vertical piazza" in the building's center.

Address: 41 Cooper Square, New York (NY) 1003, USA. **Client:** The Cooper Union. **Completion:** 2009. **Architect:** Thom Mayne/ Morphosis. **Function:** Academic building for the Advancement of Science and Art.

↑ | **Donor's signage** on the building's roof terrace engraved in granite
→ | **Optically extruded letterforms on the façade**
↓ | **Detail donor's walk**

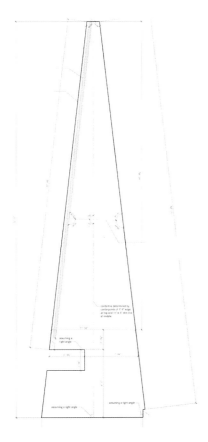

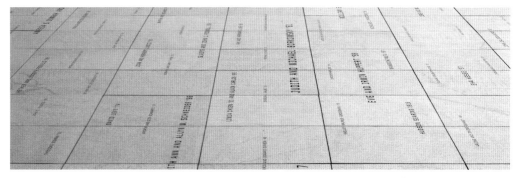

BrandCulture
Communications

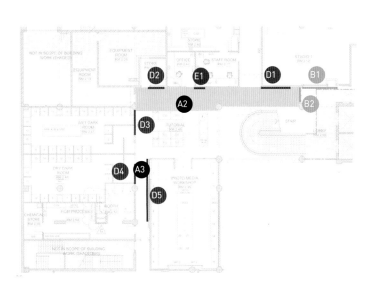

↑↑ | **Walkway** indicating machines by
number from the entry
↖ | **Floor plan with graphic concept**
↑ | **Floor graphics** influenced by the London
Underground "Tube"

UTS Find & Discover
Sydney

BrandCulture Communications were commissioned to completely revamp the design, architecture and building faculty of the University of Technology. The result is a 1,700 square
meter space with striking graphics lining the walls and floors: rooms encased with glass
panels with "molecular" graphics. The workshop is divided into three main areas: a 24-
hour studio, the laser room and the main workshop floor. As a visual tribute to modern
architecture (Herzog & de Meuron), the stretched form was created with a large dot screen
running throughout to allow for visibility. The result shows modern iconic graphic styling
with an engineering influence, featuring bold use of the flooring area.

PROJECT FACTS Location: Sydney, Australia. **Client:** University of Technology (UTS). **Completion:** 2010. **Architect:** Gardner Wetherill Associates. **Function:** 24-hour workshop studio and laser room.

↑ | Floor and wall graphics
↓ | Main workshop floor with a delineated walkway for safety

↑ | Iconic graphic featuring bold use of the flooring area

compactlab creative
consulting

↖ | **Directional signage for children**
↑↑ | **Classroom door sign for all users**
↑ | **Directional signage by staircase for adults**

Petites-Fontaines Elementary School
Geneva

"Les Petites-Fontaines" is an infants and primary school basically intended for children aged between 4 and 12, but also attended by adults. CompactLab opted to develop amusing pictograms that are easily accessible in terms of the imagination and language of children, including those who have not yet learned to read. Accordingly, the signaletic concept was expressed in the use of animal icons for the classrooms and of symbols related to school activities. Lively colors and oval shapes provided an attractive and comfortable atmosphere. The icons proved to be successful and were also used in the form of stamps to sign off class work and as stencils for outside effects. This enabled the entire school to share in an expressive visual narrative.

PROJECT FACTS

Location: Geneva, Switzerland. **Client:** Commune de Plan-les-Ouates. **Completion:** 2010. **Architect:** Atelier d'architecture Brodbeck & Roulet. **Graphic designer:** Mauren Brodbeck. **Typeface:** Cargo (Optimo) and Pixelfarm. **Function:** Elementary School.

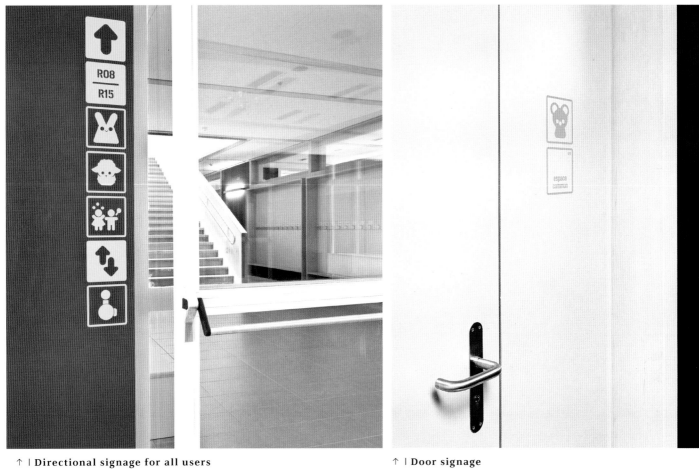

↑ | **Directional signage for all users**
↓ | **Informational signage by entrance**

↑ | **Door signage**
↑ | **Pictography**

↑↑ | Lobby with three-dimensional identi-
fication building sign "C"
↖ | Building "C" identification sign
↑ | Women's restroom sign

CAE – Center for Adult Education
Melbourne

In collaboration with Gray Puksand Architects, Fabio Ongarato Design (FOD) developed a comprehensive visual language based on information pathways, connectivity and transformation to bring a new perspective to this CAE office and learning space. The design program explored the notion of transforming lives through learning; acknowledging the transformative nature of the organization and the significance of the Melbourne CBD as part of the CAE "campus" context. FOD set a design approach expressed through a signage and environmental graphics package that explores the notion that occupants should be treated as sophisticated and intelligent learners and not just students.

Address: 278 Flinders Lane, Melbourne VIC 3000, Australia. **Client:** CAE – Center for Adult Education. **Completion:** 2009. **Architect:** Gray Pucksand Architects. **Designer and typographer:** Dan Peterson, Maurice Lai. **Function:** Adult education institution.

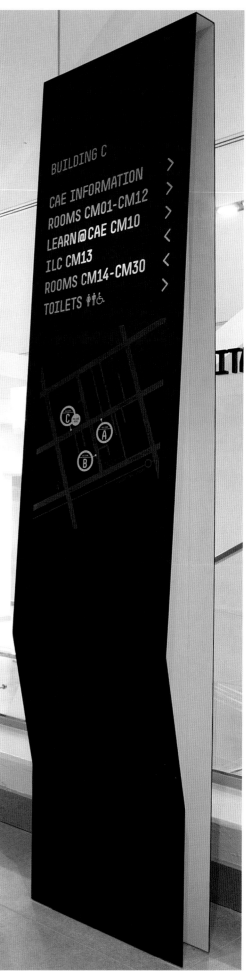

↑ | Room identification sign
→ | Directional signage and map
↓ | Three-dimensional logo sign

Naoki Terada/ Terada
Design Architects

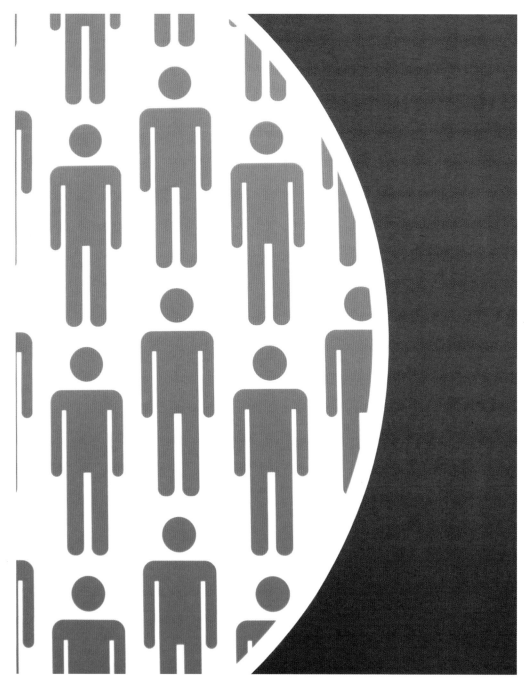

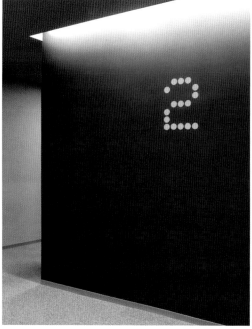

↖ | Attention-grabbing sign: men's restroom
↑↑ | Colorful wall with two-dimensional floor level sign
↑ | Locker rooms' signage indicated with a painted key on the walls

Senzoku Gakuen College of Music "Black Hall"
Kanagawa

This vibrant extension to Toyko's Senzoku Gakuen College of Music consists of "a strategic use of color", bright, eye-popping painted surfaces and large, attention-grabbing signs. The main design element is water-based acrylic paint – available in an endless range of brilliant hues – to brighten the extension, known as the "Black Hall", which accommodates the school's newly established department of rock and pop music. The 6,300 square meter interior includes recording studios, multimedia studios and classrooms for students who play the electronic organ and practice rooms with sealed windows.

Address: 2-3-1 Hisamoto, Takatsu-ku, Kawasaki-shi, Kanagawa 213-8580, Japan. **Client:** Senzoku Gakuen College of Music. **Completion:** 2009. **Architect:** Nihon Sekkei. **Function:** Music college.

↑ | **Main floor door indicating room numbers**
↓ | **Interior, fourth floor**

↑ | **Water graphic sign**
↓ | **Diagrammatic second floor plan**

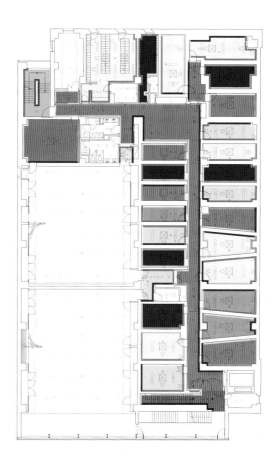

Jens Könen,
Kristin Stratmann

↖↖ | Signage in corridor
↖ | Directional signage
↑↑ | DIN A6 postcard, informational signage
↑ | Room signage

Von Da Nach B
Münster

The signage system "Von Da Nach B" was created for the new building of the faculty of design of Münster University of Applied Sciences. It deliberately integrates the user into the process of orientation and allows them to take the covering of the distance in their own hand and information along the way. The basic design medium is a postcard with a DIN A6 standard format. In this way, three stations with orientational, informational features form a flexible overall system.

PROJECT FACTS
Location: Münster, Germany. **Client:** University Fachhochschule Münster. **Completion:** 2009. **Function:** University.

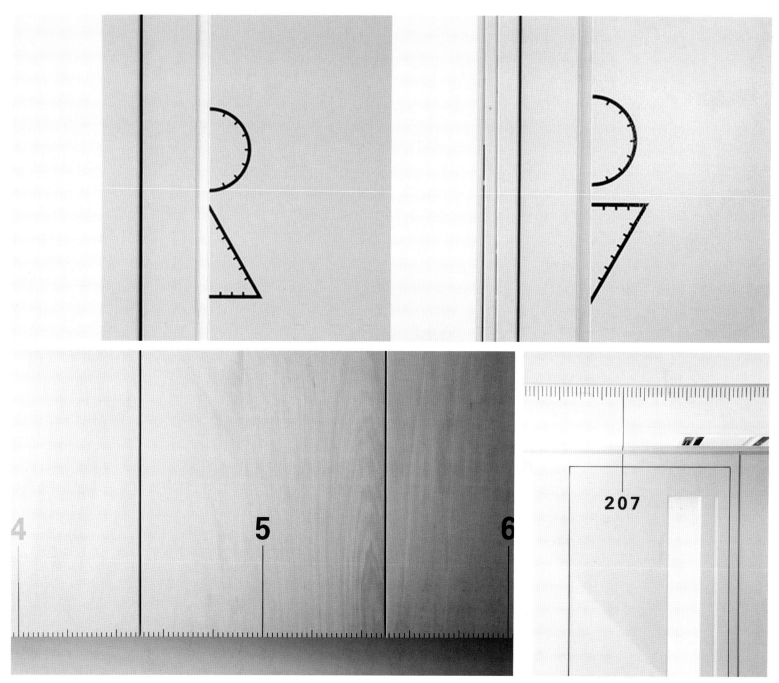

↑↑ | Girls' and boys' bathroom sign
↑ | Measuring scale indicating cabinet numbers
↗ | Measuring scale indicating room number

Scales
Tokyo

Scales is the signage design for a private cramming school for children. Units of measurement were used as the motif; measuring the growth achieved was the concept behind the signs. For example, the columns at the entrance resemble the scale of the nine size units (centimeters, yard, feet, inches, etc...). Children can learn unfamiliar scales while measuring their height. Scales is a theme where the design and space fuse with the measurements.

PROJECT FACTS
Location: Tokyo, Japan. **Completion:** 2010. **Function:** Cram school.

Paula Scher/ Pentagram

↑↑ | Motivational slogans
↖ | Motivational slogans
↑ | Exterior façade with view to interior
graphics

Achievement First Endeavor Middle School

Brooklyn, New York

For the Achievement First Endeavor Middle School, a charter school for grades fifth
through eighth in Brooklyn, Pentagram created a program of environmental graphics that
help the school interiors become a vibrant space for learning. The project was completed in
collaboration with Rogers Marvel Architects, who designed the school as a refurbishment
and expansion of an existing building. The environmental graphics at the school have been
inspired by a series of motivational slogans used by its teachers. Achievement First origi-
nally produced these slogans as colorful stickers that students were encouraged to affix to
their books and lockers. The designers enlarged these into supergraphics that define the
interior spaces and help the building become a participant in the learning process.

PROJECT FACTS

Address: 510 Waverly Avenue, Brooklyn (NY) 11238, USA. **Client:** Achievement First. **Completion:** 2010. **Art director and designer:** Paula Scher. **Architects:** Rogers Marvel Architects. **Overall signage and production:** Denise J. Mayer Architectural Graphics. **Supergraphic lettering:** Nela Design. **Graphic striping:** Claridan Contracting. **Typology:** Education. **Function:** Middle School.

↑ | Quotations run around the walls of the gym
↓ | Gymnasium with slogans hanging as pictures

↑ | Graphics in the main staircase

R2 design

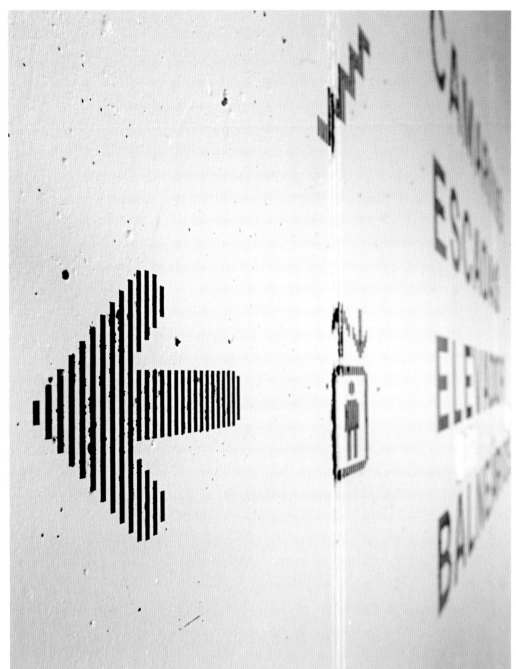

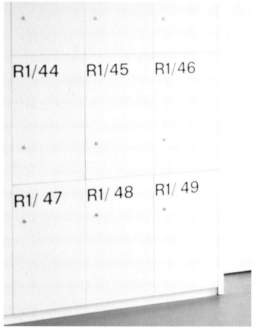

↖ | Detail of directional, black painted signage
↑↑ | Level sign in landing between stairs
↑ | Lockers' number

Quinta das Flores
Secondary School
Coimbra

The design brief called for new signage system that was innovative yet functional, inexpensive to realize, and integrated with the new architecture. Given the campus' accommodation of a conservatory, the designers decided to focus on the school's unique relationship to music as a starting point for the design. Inspired by the visualization of sound waves as repetitive lines, as well as the verticality of the façade windows, they created a base type comprised of vertical strips and a series of pictograms that also allude to sound. The idea of sound intensity was translated into the design by differentiating the density of the typeface according to the numerical value of the level of the building on which it is situated.

PROJECT FACTS

Address: Rua Pedro Nunes, 3030-199 Coimbra, Portugal. **Completion:** 2010. **Graphic design and type-face architecture:** José Paulo do Santos. **Function:** Artistic School of Music.

← | Large scale floor level (1) in landing between stairs
↓ | Directional signage

Büro für Gestaltung
Wangler & Abele

↖ I **Identity sign on glazed façade**
↑ I **Logos in three different colors**

Campus Vest
Recklinghausen

The logo for this grouping of vocational colleges and sports hall derives from the alignment of the actual buildings to each other in plan. In this way a common identity is achieved for the new campus, while still preserving the individual identities of the elements within it. As each of the three buildings had distinct color concepts for Abeile fixtures and fittings, three-color ranges were chosen for the design. Key information and coding is displayed on white panels painted directly onto the wall surfaces. The subtle color nuances on the different levels add a light touch but also play a role in orientation. At the entrance area of each of the institutions, their individual identity is underlined by portraits and biographies of their respective founders, with large-print letters spelling out their names.

PROJECT FACTS

Adress: Campus Vest 3, 45665 Recklinghausen, Germany. **Completion:** 2008. **Architect:** scholl architekten scholl.balbach.walker. **Function:** Vocational college.

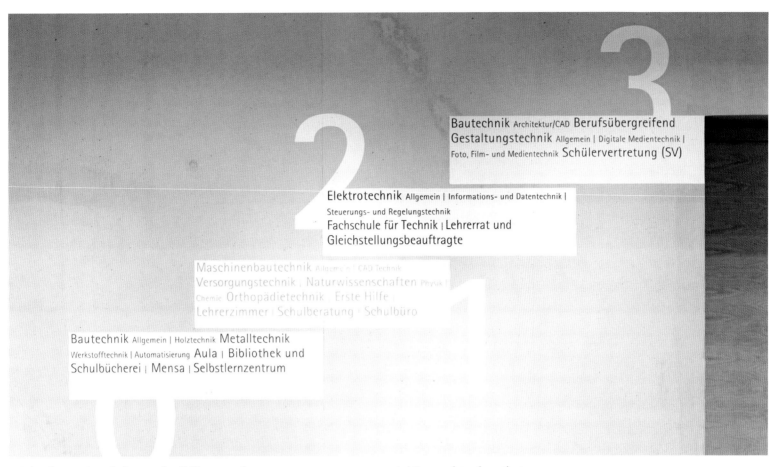

Bautechnik Architektur/CAD Berufsübergreifend
Gestaltungstechnik Allgemein | Digitale Medientechnik |
Foto, Film- und Medientechnik Schülervertretung (SV)

Elektrotechnik Allgemein | Informations- und Datentechnik |
Steuerungs- und Regelungstechnik
Fachschule für Technik | Lehrerrat und
Gleichstellungsbeauftragte

Maschinenbautechnik Allgemein | CAD Technik
Versorgungstechnik | Naturwissenschaften Physik |
Chemie Orthopädietechnik | Erste Hilfe |
Lehrerzimmer | Schulberatung | Schulbüro

Bautechnik Allgemein | Holztechnik Metalltechnik
Werkstofftechnik | Automatisierung Aula | Bibliothek und
Schulbücherei | Mensa | Selbstlernzentrum

↑ | Informational signage in different colors
↓ | Floor level 3 sign painted directly onto wall surface

↓ | Room sign changing room

0.27
1a

Umkleiden

sh 0.27

2.stock süd netthoevel
& gaberthüel

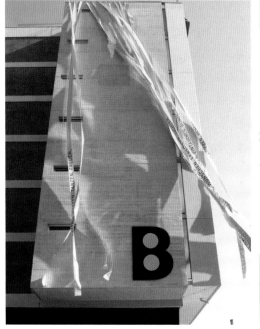

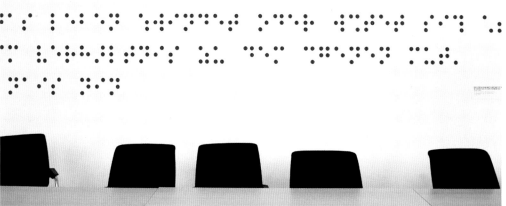

ⰧⰧ | Exterior identity sign
↑↑ | Entry sign on glass sliding doors
Ⱗ | Façade sign
↑ | Classroom with Braile font on wall

Center for Blind and Handicapped People
Bern

For more than 125 years this facility's name was "help for seeing". The designers developed a distinctive character from the original name to create a new name, corporate design and signage design for the Center for Blind and Handicapped People in Bern. The letter "B" combined with the letter "B" in the Braille font defines the new sign for the center. The tactile points and the colors unmistakably remind the seeing of "blind". Besides the clear symbol and the name, the claim "side by side with people:" is the element of communication. It works with large typography and Braille. The ergonomic nameplates inscriptions signs are tactile and appear in standard size. These metal plates were produced economically with raised fonts using conventional technology.

PROJECT FACTS **Location:** Bern, Switzerland. **Completion:** 2010. **Function:** Center for blind and handicapped people.

91

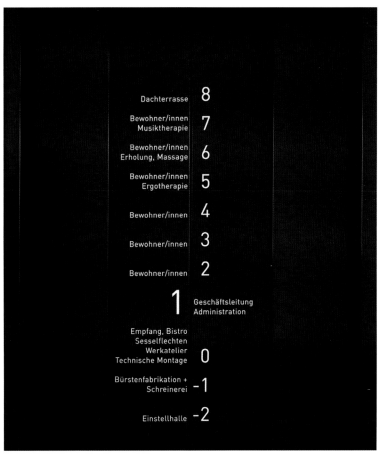

↑ | Smoking room sign on door
↓ | Hallway with room numbers indicated along the wall

↑ | Elevator signage
↓ | Painted room numbers
↓↓ | Room number sign in letters and in Braile

HEALTH /
SPORTS / LEISURE

Sortie
Consultation d'urgence pédiatrique
Cabinets médicaux

↑ | **Parking lot assigned numbers**

K Clinic
Nabari Mie

The clinic is located along the main road of the town and made of steel tube structure. The cantilever of the upper floating part is 17 meters long due to the "monocoque" structure that is composed of steel panel t6 and steel deck plate. The shape of the building reflects linearity and inclination of the main road and eventually tries to reify the missing profile of the land. The lower part contains the clinic and the upper part is the doctor's study. The parking signage was designed with large scale numbers and pictograms, following the angle of the main road, just like the building itself.

↑ | Parking pictograms
↓ | Building at an angle, the same as the
parking lot

↑ | Interior view

Büro North

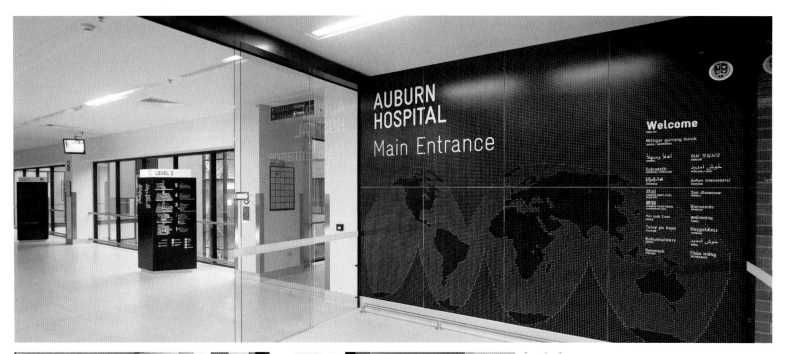

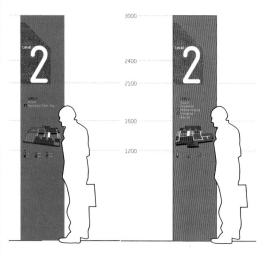

↑↑ | **Lobby wall signage**
↖ | **Entrance directory**
↑ | **Level and map sign**

Auburn Hospital
Sydney

Auburn Hospital is a 120-bed acute care health facility on the eastern border of Sydney West Area Health Service. Büro North was enlisted to create signage design for this complex, busy and stressful hospital environment. A strict color palette was chosen to work with all the interiors and with the overall hospital theming while maintaining a high level of legibility and wayfinding function. Pattern was employed as a visual language to strengthen and coordinate with the hospital's overall theme and art.

PROJECT FACTS

Address: Hargrave Road, Auburn, Sydney, Australia. **Client:** Brookfield Multiplex. **Completion:** 2009. **Function:** Hospital.

↑ | Lift lobby portal sign
↓ | Entrance directory

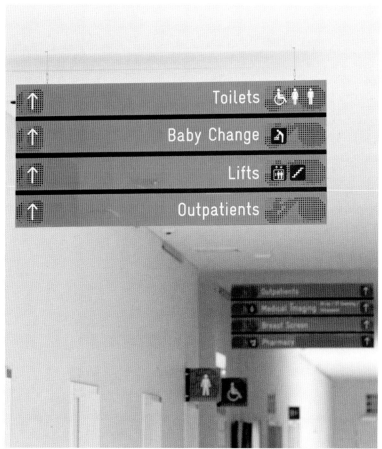

↑ | Directional signage suspended from ceiling

büro uebele
visuelle kommunikation

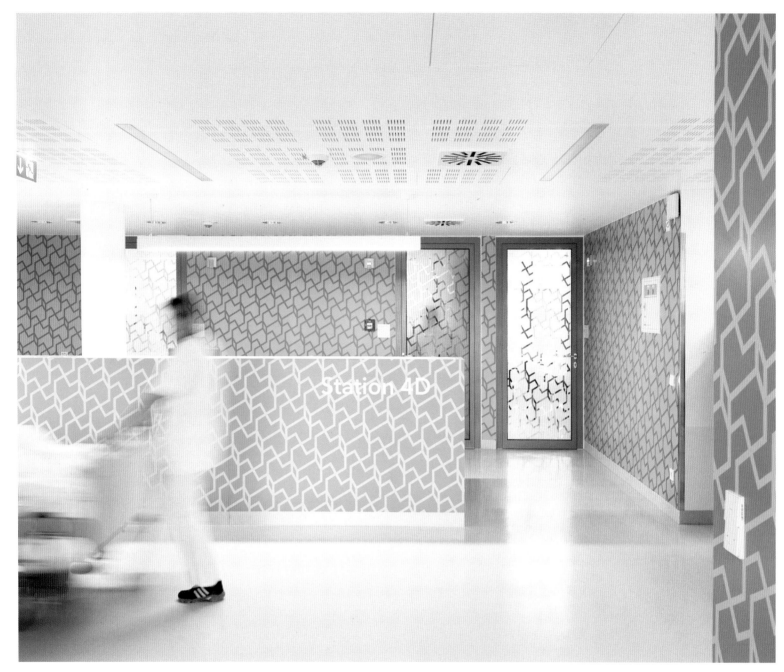

↑ | Colored, patterned wallpaper

Signage System, Offenbach Hospital

Offenbach am Main

Geometrical colored patterns guide visitors to their destination and lighten the mood of this sterile setting. Each of the numerous locations has its own combination of pattern and color to set it apart, and then each visitor is able to identify "their" color and pattern that will guide them through the hospital complex. The reception areas are identified by large areas of characteristically colored, patterned wallpaper, with identical designs on the counters and doors. This visual coding gives these areas their own distinct identity. The system is based on a highly flexible concept that can be easily and quickly modified.

Location: Offenbach am Main, Germany. **Client:** Klinikum Offenbach GmbH. **Completion:** 2010. **Product design:** ZieglerBürg Büro für Gestaltung. **Architect:** woernerundpartner. **Function:** Hospital.

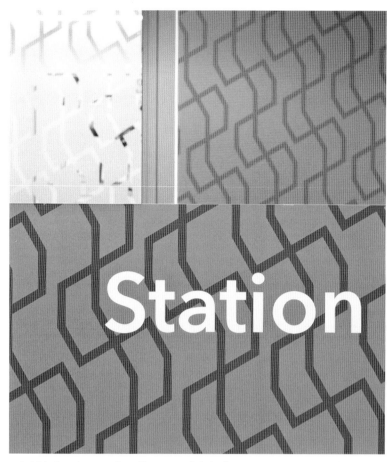

↑ | Pink patterned wallpaper with infor-
mational signage (station)
↓ | Informational signage coding at
entrance

↑ | Interior signage

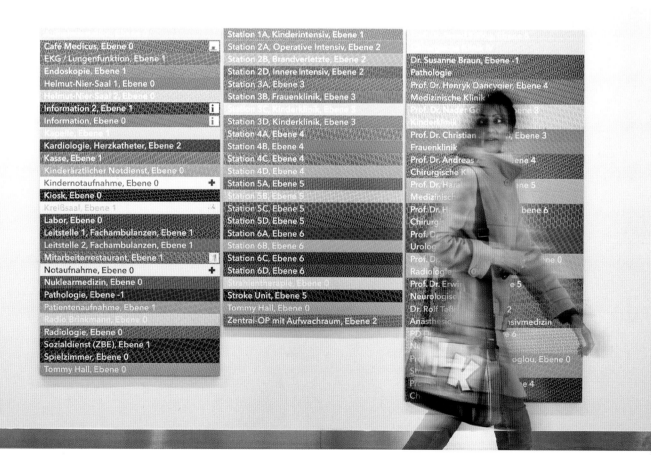

compactlab creative
consulting

↖↖ | Stair indicational sign on glass surface
↖ | Waiting room sign
↑ | Detail of restroom sign

Pediatric Emergency Clinic Grangettes
Geneva

This unique children's emergency center has a discreet and effective control system which blends harmoniously into the architecture of the building and incorporates the principle of the visual identity of the clinic. All icons have been specifically developed for this purpose.

PROJECT FACTS

Location: Geneva, Switzerland. **Client:** Fondation Hans Wilsdorf & Clinique des Grangettes. **Completion:** 2009. **Function:** Pediatric emergency clinic.

↑ | **Meeting room sign on door**
↓ | **Exit (Sortie) sign**

↑ | **Sign to restrooms**

↖ | Main entrance signage on the wall
↑↑ | Consultation room
↑ | Hallway with floor signage

Beckmann and Ehlers Cardiology Practice
Berlin

A little red dot pulses like a heartbeat, while the initials "BE" become the new trademark of Beckmann and Ehlers's cardiology practice in Berlin. Various letterheads associating the initials with other terms, such as "BENACHRICHTIGUNG" ("notice") or "BEFUND" ("result"), help to individualize stationary for every occasion, and a special printing technique further provides a unique effect. Referred patients also have access to a specially developed address list of other cardiologists, including all relevant information.

PROJECT FACTS
Location: Berlin, Germany. **Completion:** 2009. **Function:** Cardiology Practice.

103

↑ | Registration area (Empfang), signage
on glass
↓ | Red signage letters on the floor

↑ | Waiting area and laboratory

PLAYFRAME
Agentur für Kommunikation

↑ | Thematic wall illustration indicating
room numbers

Therapy from Head to Toe
Berlin

Different medical doctors underneath one roof – this up-and-coming model of medical practice is reflected in the "Patient Practice" logo. The logo is composed of letters in different typographical designs and symbolizes the individuality of the patients. With the help of a well thought-out signage system serving as thematic wall illustration at the same time, the patient is systematically guided through the facilities. A red floor, handmade seat benches, and light-flooded rooms create a modern and friendly atmosphere instilling trust and giving patients the good feeling to receive competent advice in the practice.

PROJECT FACTS

Address: Tempelhofer Damm 158–160, 12099 Berlin, Germany. **Client:** Patientenpraxis, Berlin. **Completion:** 2009. **Graphic design:** Melanie Ickert, Mandy Binder. **Illustration:** Katarina Kreutzberg, Melanie Ickert. **Function:** Medical clinic.

↑ | **Graphical signage**
↓ | **Overhead signage above registration desk**

Mind Design

↖↖ | **Consultation room number**
↖ | **Identification sign at registration desk**
↑ | **Door hinge graphic**

D100
London

D100 is a modern dentistry at the Barbican (100 Aldersgate street). The identity is inspired by the raking patterns around stones in Japanese Zen gardens and protective layers of enamel around teeth. The pattern have also been applied to the interior going around furniture and various fixed or removable object in the practice.

PROJECT FACTS

Address: 100 Aldersgate Street, London EC1A 4JR, United Kingdom. **Completion:** 2009. **Function:** Dentistry.

Welcome to
Dentistry 100

↑ | Coat hanger graphic sign
↓ | Light switch graphic sign and toilet
sign

↑ | Sign at entrance

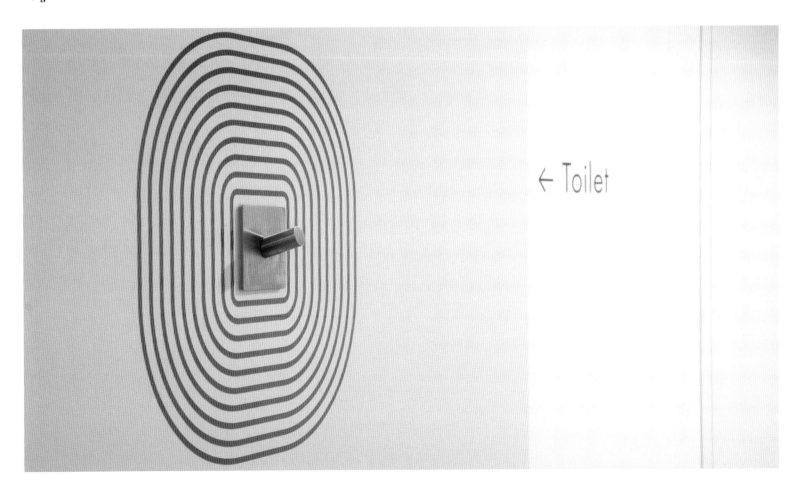

← Toilet

Gourdin & Müller

↑ | **Door and wall signage with letters broken down as lined forms**

Industrieschule Chemnitz Sports Hall
Chemnitz

The conversion of the sports hall of the Industrieschule Chemnitz vocational school offered an opportunity to realize a new signage concept, including guidance. Used primarily by the educational center, the guidance system addresses a young and open public. One characteristic element of the guidance system is the graphic interpretation of the lettering. The breakdown of the letters as lined forms establishes a thematic connection to the sporting environment. Both the expression of dynamism and the typical marking of lines and playing areas are reflected in the typography modified for the project. The pictogram system created for this forms a visual extension of the lettering, with which it is not only combined, but also interconnected.

PROJECT FACTS
Location: Chemnitz, Germany. **Client:** City of Chemnitz, Construction Office. **Completion:** 2010.
Function: Sports hall.

↑ | **Pictogram system is a visual extension of the lettering**
↓ | **Restroom signs**

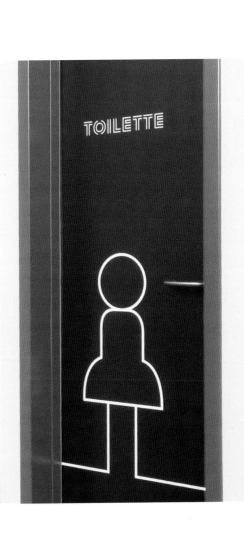

← | Painted directional signage
↓ | Door pictograms

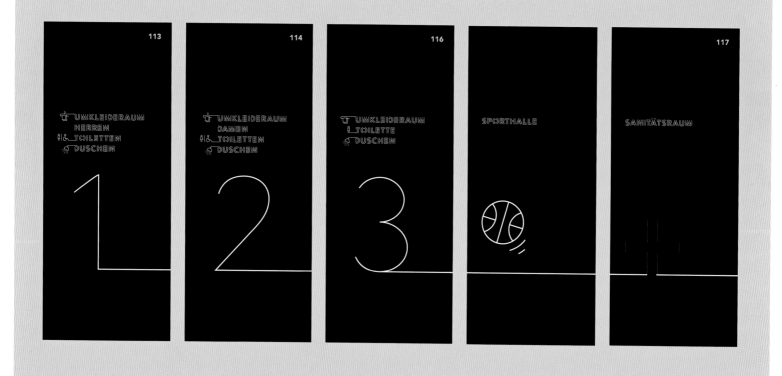

← | Detail of door signage
↓ | Pictograms

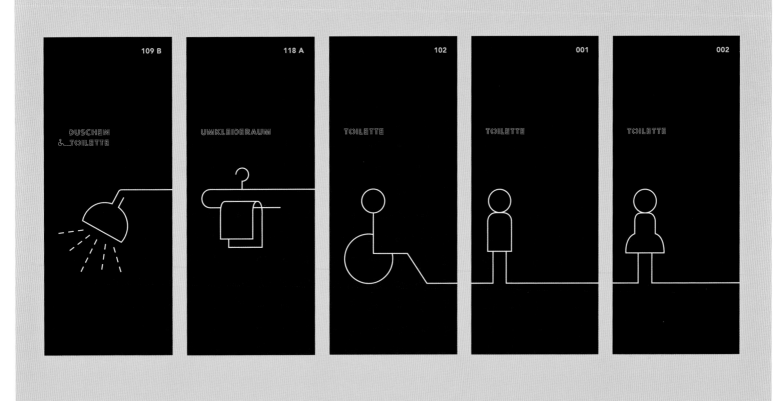

Michael Bierut and Michael Gericke/ Pentagram

ꜛꜛ | Main entrance featuring louvers with graphics of Jets' captains
↑↑ | Lobby with three-dimensional identification building sign "C"
↑↑ | Front desk at the entrance with sign
ꜛ | Identification signage at the entrance
↑ | New York Jets Curtis Martin MVP wall

New York Jets Training Center
New York

Michael Gericke and his team at Pentagram designed a bold program of environmental graphics that fosters a sense of pride, focus and competition for everyone associated with the NFL team. Pentagram has worked with the Jets since 2002 on the development of its graphic identity, including a custom typeface called Jets Bold designed by Hoefler & Frere-Jones that is used in all communications. The graphics have become part of the team DNA, and at the training center they are integrated into the architecture to create an environment that carries the spirit of the Jets onto the training field.

Location: Florham Park, New Jersey (NJ), USA. **Client:** New York Jets. **Completion:** 2010. **Architect:** Skidmore, Owings & Merrill. **Function:** Training center.

↑ | Supergraphics in stairwell
↓ | Team auditorium with dimensional signage

↑ | Team stairwell with supergraphic slogans

↖ | Informational signage, third level
↑↑ | Detail room's sign
↑ | Doors' frame signs

Bota Bota Spa
Montreal

Bota Bota is the new name given to a 20-meters-long ferryboat that used to link Sorel and Berthier in the 1950s and that is been retrofitted into a five-level floating spa that includes saunas, baths, massage and other treatment rooms, a cafe, and an outdoor terrace. The boat's architecture, redesign and visual identity are a collaborative effort between Sid Lee Architecture and Sid Lee. The 670 pre-fabricated portholes provide graphic interest while leveraging the panoramic and relaxing views of the city. The marine markers identity concept is unique; using a visual language characterized by pure, simple lines, the spa brings markers of the marine world to its logo, signage and stationery.

Address: 358 de la Commune West, Quays of the Old Port, Montreal, Canada. **Client:** Bota Bota, Spa-sur-l'eau. **Completion:** 2010. **Architect:** Sid Lee Architecture. **Function:** Spa.

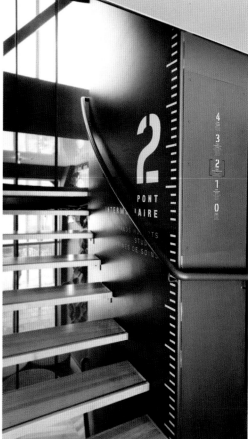

↑ | Locker room with large scale letter signs
↓ | Informational signage by staircase, fourth level

↑ | Informational signage, second floor
↓ | Detail font

Büro für Gestaltung
Wangler & Abele

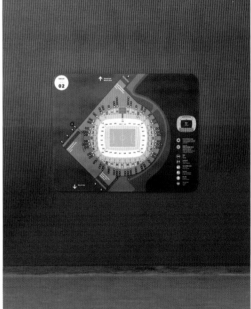

↖ | Informational signage, blue zone
↑↑ | Color circles serve as directional
signage
↑ | Site map

Green Point Stadium
Cape Town

The design refers to the urban district of Green Point in Cape Town. The central element is
the circle serving as a basis for all information, coding, directions, colors and pictograms.
The circular elements can be combined freely, vertically or horizontally, in columns or
rows. Due to its reduced form, the circle clearly stands out from the background and the
surrounding architecture. It is therefore very suitable as information carrier and it serves
as an economical solution in terms of manufacture.

Location: Cape Town, South Africa. **Client:** Stadium Architects. **Completion:** 2010. **Architects:** gmp Architekten von Gerkan, Marg und Partner, Berlin, Point Architects & Urban Designers, Cape Town. **Function:** Stadium.

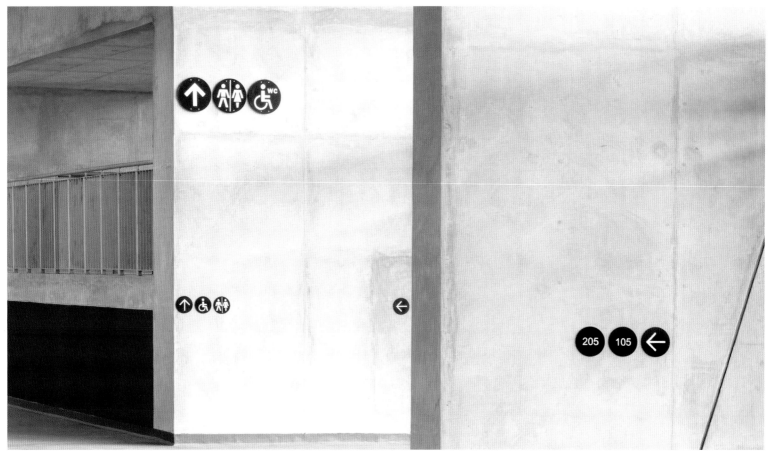

↑ | Black circle signs with pictograms, tactile signs within easy reach
↓ | Directional signage, circle signs

↓ | Directional signs indicating coat room and handicapped access way

↑↑ | **Exterior signage**
↑ | **Logo**
↗ | **Informational signage on glass surface**

Znips
London

Identity for Znips, a hair and beauty salon in Central London. The logo is inspired by locks of hair and hand-cut lettering found in an 80's Punk fanzine. As part of the interior a piece of wall art was designed from chopped books resembling curled strands of hair and the curved shapes of the logo.

PROJECT FACTS
Location: London, United Kingdom. **Completion:** 2009. **Function:** Hair and beauty salon.

Büro für Gestaltung
Wangler & Abele

↑↑ | Bright signs at entrance
↗↗ | Identity sign at entry way
↑ | Restrooms' supergraphics and seating section number
↗ | Letter sections' signs

Moses-Mabhida Stadium Durban
Durban

The design for the visual communication at Moses Mabhida Stadium in Durban is inspired by themes found in the region: contemporary art, tradition, crafts and everyday culture. Bright, rich ornamestaltung, geometric lines and a warm, strong palette of colors derive easily from the climate, landscape and vegetation. Line structures and texts are applied direct to surfaces, echoing local traditions of decorating, painting and illustrating all manner of things. At the same time, this method aligns well with cost-efficiency considerations.

PROJECT FACTS
Location: Durban, South Africa. **Client:** Ibhola Lethu Architects, Durban. **Completion:** 2010. **Architects:** Theunissen Jankowitz Architects. **Function:** Stadium.

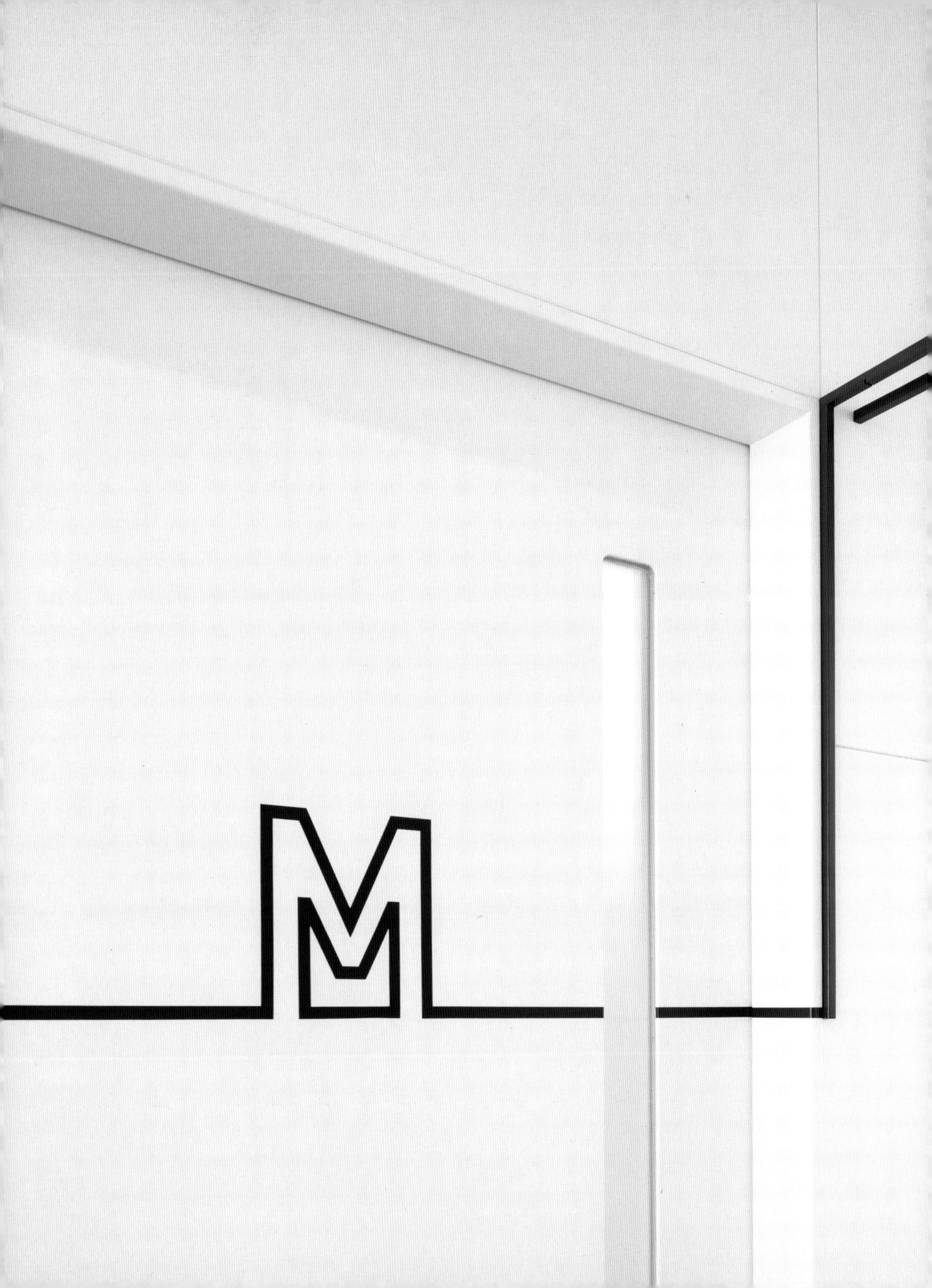
M

HOSPITALITY / RETAIL / GASTRONOMY

Hiromura Design Office

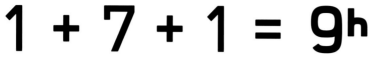

 Shower   Sleep   Rest   9 hours

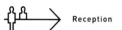 Reception 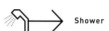 Shower  Lounge

 Locker 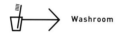 Washroom 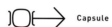 Capsule

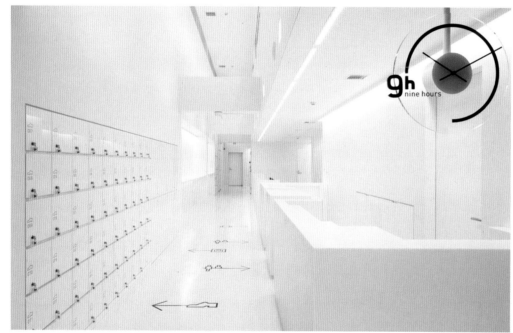

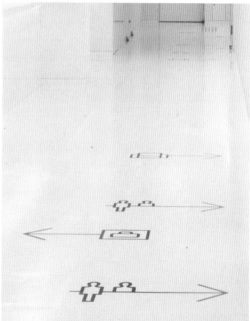

↖↖ | Design concept
↑↑ | Elevators service both women's and men's capsules
↖ | Lobby with lockers
↑ | Lobby with pictograms painted on floor

9h nine hours
Kyoto

9h nine hours is an original type of a stay-hotel called "Transit Stay", based on the idea of 1h (shower) + 7h (sleep) + 1h (dressing). 9h, where people stay in a capsule unit, was created to become an infrastructure in urban limited space, and it suggests a new style of a stay-hotel with its original design. Graphic, interior and product designers had shared the concept and ideas from the beginning of the plan, and every single piece of the facility was designed from the ground up. In terms of the signage system, the pictograms on a wall and a floor explain how to use facilities, which is easy for foreigners to understand as well.

PROJECT FACTS **Address:** 588 Teianmaeno-cho Shijo Teramachi, Shimogyo-ku Kyoto, Japan. **Client:** Cubic Corporation. **Completion:** 2009. **Creative direction and product design:** Fumie Shibata. **Sign and graphic design:** Masaaki Hiromura. **Interior design:** Takaaki Nakamura. **Function:** Hotel.

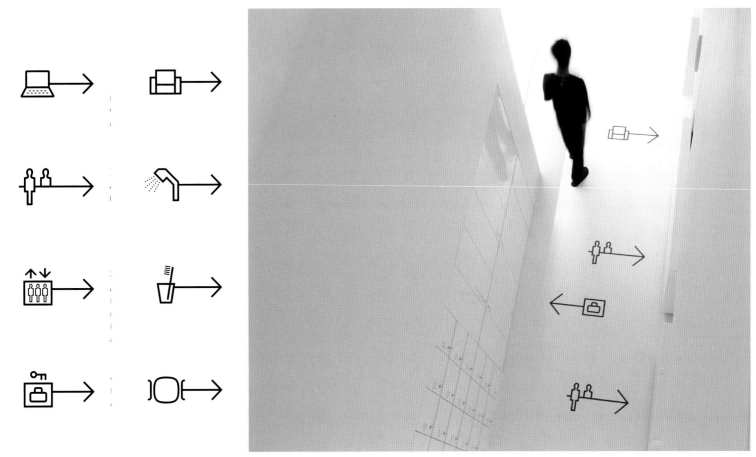

↑ | Pictograms indicating different uses
↓ | Sleeping capsules' numbers on the floor
↗ | Aerial view to hallway with pictograms on the floor

Fabio Ongarato Design

↖ | Maze restaurant signage
↑↑ | Sky bar signage
↑ | Directional signage, restrooms

Crown Metropol Hotel
Melbourne

Crown Metropol, the third hotel in the Crown Entertainment Complex, consists of 658 rooms, making it the largest hotel in Australia fand the first under the Crown umbrella to cater for a more urban business and leisure clientele. With architecture designed by Bates Smart Architects, Fabio Ongarato Design was responsible for the name, brand identity, print collateral and signage design for not only the hotel but also "28", the exclusive sky bar on Level 28 and residential spa "ISIKA". The graphic language and visual identities for these new urban leisure destinations reflect a quiet, personal sophistication, in keeping with its architectural aspirations.

PROJECT FACTS
Address: 8 Whiteman Street, Southbank Melbourne Victoria 3006, Australia. **Client:** Crown. **Completion:** 2010. **Architect:** Bates Smart Architects. **Function:** Hotel.

↑ | Directional sigange to casino, services and car garage
↓ | Sign room number

↑ | Hotel lobby signage
↓ | Exterior signage

Frost* Design

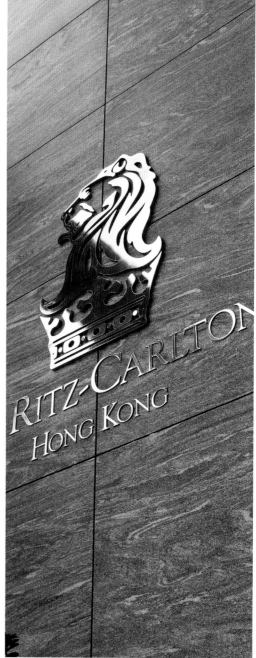

↖↖ | **Exterior sign**
↖ | **Bronze metal folded concierge sign**
↑ | **Logo and identification sign**

The Ritz-Carlton
Hong Kong

The Ritz-Carlton has made a dramatic return to the Hong Kong skyline: occupying the top 16 floors of the landmark 118-story International Commerce Center in Kowloon, it is the world's tallest hotel. Developer Sun Hung-Kai Sun asked Frost* Design for an identification and an intuitive wayfinding system that would reflect both the venerable hotelier's past and its highrising aspirations. The designers created a jewel-like motif that mirrors the effortless sophistication of the finest luxury brands. The key signage elements were drawn from a ribbon of bronzed metal folded to create form. The approach blends with the contours of the hotel's textured environment of timbers and natural stones.

Address: International Commerce Center, 1 Austin Road West, Kowloon, Hong Kong, China. **Client:** SHKP Hotels. **Completion:** 2011. **Function:** Hotel.

LADIES

GENTLEMEN

RESTROOM

↑ | Typical facilities typography and pictograms
↓ | Identification sign

↑ | Bronze metal folded wellness area sign

↑ | Guest rooms' directional signs
← | Typical bilingual signage panel

SPRINKLER & DRENCH CONTROL VALVE

—

花灑和
水簾系統控制閥機房

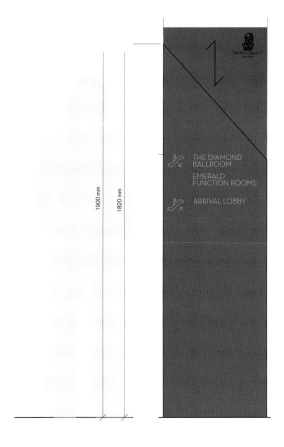

↑ | Construction drawing showing directional totem signage
← | Library sign printed on glass surface

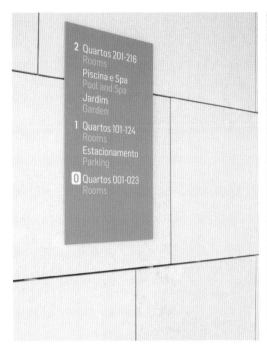

↖↖ | Informational signage in exterior staircase, painted on metal plate
↑↑ | Pool information sign, painted mill cut acrylic
↖ | Garden informational sign
↑ | Three-dimensional painted metal pictograms for terrace and restrooms

Estoi Palace Pousada
Faro

Signage for a luxury charm hotel. The Estoi Palace Pousada is a hotel of the Pousadas de Portugal group, a chain of luxury hotels in Portugal. The hotel is located in a magnificent palace from the 18th century and combines historical and modern stylistic elements in a reserved way. The discreetly designed orientation and information system guides guests through the elegant spaces and outdoor facilities which adapt to the location.

PROJECT FACTS

Address: Rua de São José, 8005-465 Faro, Portugal. **Client:** Gonçalo Byrne Arquitectos. **Completion:** 2010. **Art direction:** João Bicker. **Design:** Rita Marquito. **Signage assessment:** Cristina Catarino. **Project management:** Alexandre Matos. **Function:** Hotel.

↑ | Three-dimensional directional signage in guestrooms' corridor
↓ | Directional signage painted on parking garage's wall

↑ | Three-dimensional informational signage in interior staircase
↓ | Parking exit sign and pictograms painted on structural columns

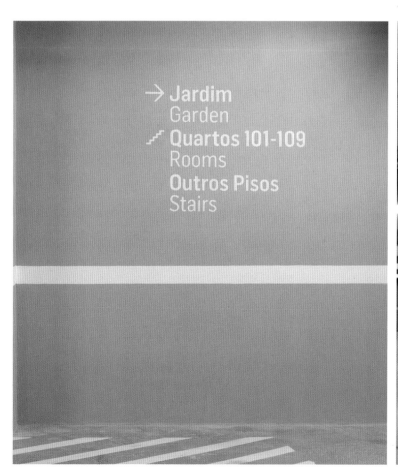

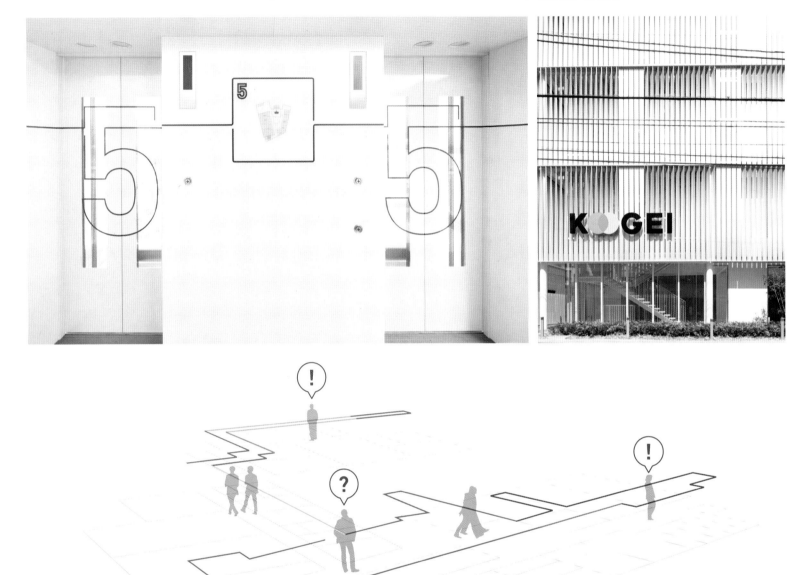

↖↖ | 5th floor elevator signage runs from wall to wall
↑↑ | Front façade sign
↑ | Conceptual drawing

Tokyo Polytechnic University New Dormitories
Tokyo

Tokyo Polytechnic University's Nakano campus, which previously focused primarily on photography, recently underwent a major facelift. Dubbed a "media arts center," the new building is home to all genres of media arts, both new and old, including photography, motion graphics, interactive design, gaming, among other creative majors. The signage design concept is based on an "info-line": all information, such as room numbers, navigation signage and so on, is organized on a single line throughout the interior. By creating a system with different information and making it clear for the users to navigate the space in an effective way, the single line also works as effective visual identity of the dormitories.

PROJECT FACTS
Location: Tokyo, Japan. **Client:** Tokyo Polytechnic Universtity. **Completion:** 2010. **Architect:** Sakakura Associates. **Sign design:** Masaaki Hiromura. **Function:** Student dormitories.

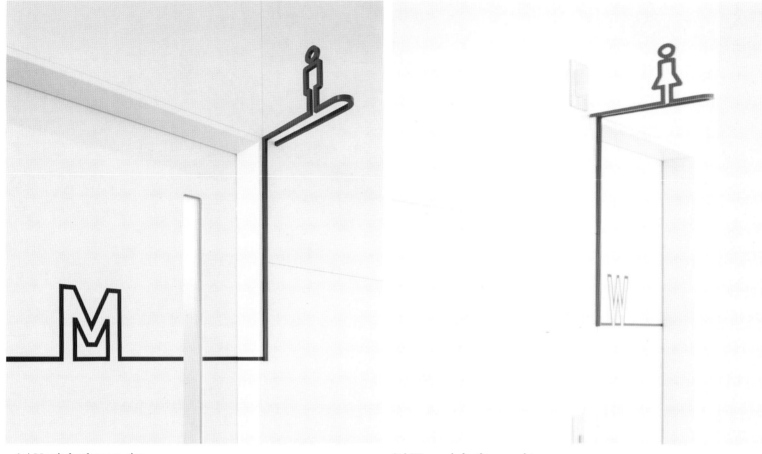

↑ | Men's bathroom sign
↓ | Dormitories with signage on the door in Japanese and English

↑ | Women's bathroom sign

Gabor Palotai Design

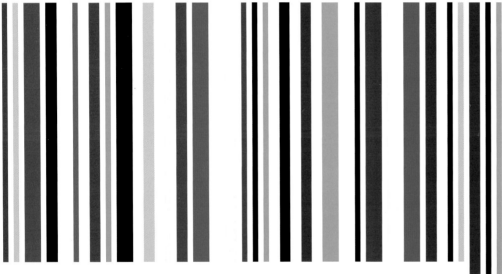

SOLLENTUNA CENTRUM

Sollentuna Centrum
Stockholm

ꜛꜛ | Detail façade sign
ꜛ | Shopping center logo
↑ | Pictograms

The Sollentuna Centrum is one of Stockholm's largest shopping centers with about 120 stores and 1,500 parking spaces. It is Sweden's first designer-oriented shopping center. It has a unique layout with four distinct shopping areas, each with its own means of expression with color, design and retail mix. The multi-coloured bar code is the DNA of the graphic profile for Sollentuna Cetrum. It embraces all brands and trends, goods and services, available at the centre in the abstraction of lines. Playful and sharp, the lines are redesigned into patterns, numbers, and pictograms, creating a vivid profile integrated into the architecture and present in every part of the shopping centre's visual communication.

PROJECT FACTS
Address: Sollentunavägen 163, Sollentuna, Sweden. **Client:** Steen & Strøm AB. **Completion:** 2010. **Art director and graphic design:** Garbor Palotai. **Graphic design:** Fredrik Söder. **Function:** Shopping center.

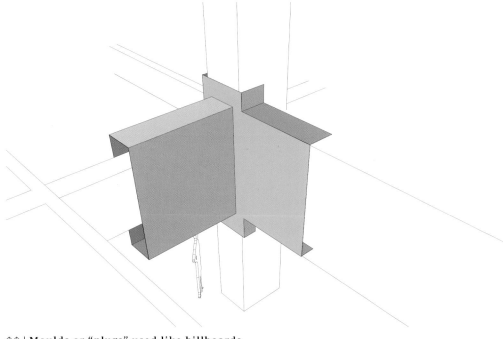

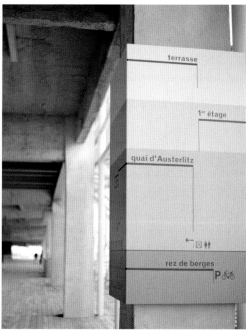

↑↑ | **Moulds or "plugs" used like billboards**
↑ | **Detail of concrete structure as a**
support for the signage system
↗ | **Signage wrapped around concrete**
columns

Docks en Seine, signage intervention
Paris

The signage intervention plays with the usual needs of signage and with the context. The building participates in the urban renewal of the 13th district of Paris. The goal of this signage project is to punctuate this horizontal movement with "beacons", and to create a declension on four levels from the access at the bank level of the Seine towards the rooftop. The preservation of the existing building keeping the concrete structure, offers support for the signage system.

PROJECT FACTS
Address: 13 Quai d'Austerlitz, 75013 Paris, France. **Client:** Icade. **Completion:** 2009. **Architect:** Jakob + MacFarlane. **Graphic designer:** Fanny Naranjo. **Function:** Fashion school, shopping center, exhibition hall and restaurants.

Gourdin & Müller

↑↑ | Overhead parking directional sign
↖ | Informational signage, ground floor
↑ | Graphic number, first floor

Centrum Galerie Dresden
Dresden

The Centrum Galerie is one of the largest inner-city shopping centers in Germany. The architectural design of Peter Kulka integrates the characteristic sculptured aluminium honeycomb of the original 1978 department store into the new façade. The aim is for the signage system to blend into the unique architecture while at the same time satisfying all functional requirements. Taking reference from the refracted form of the honeycomb on the exterior façade and the restrained black and white color scheme of the architecture, monochrome, faceted information bearers with backlit lettering were designed. The black background contrasts with the light information, with its blurred contours reminiscent of neon advertising. They form a visual unit with the selected font and the pictogram system.

PROJECT FACTS

Address: Prager Straße 15, 01069 Dresden, Germany. **Client:** Multi Development Germany GmbH. **Completion:** 2009. **Function:** Shopping center.

↑ | Overhead directional sign: restroom
and locker room
↓ | Pictograms

↑ | Informational signage, 4th level
↓ | Informational signage, ground level

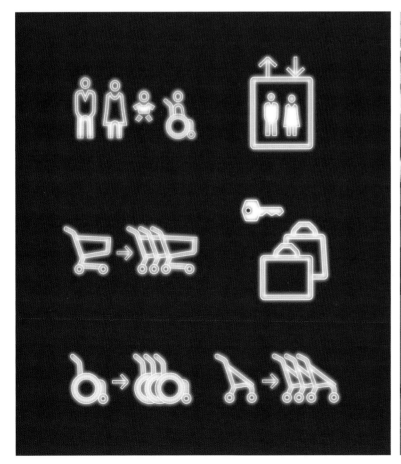

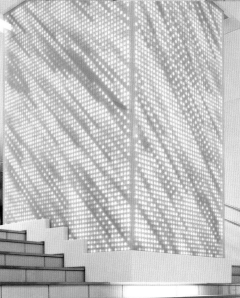

↖ | View to pillar with LED time display
↑↑ | Information counter with lit sign
↑ | Pillar with LED graphic display

Seibu Ikebukuro Flagship Store "Hikari No Tokei" Gate
Kyoto

"Hikari no tokei" or clock of light is a symbolic signage for the new entrance at the Seibu Ikebukuro flagship store. The clock is located on all four sides of a large pillar, consisting of four giant LED surfaces. These displays show the current time in an array of motion-typography and the pattern of typography changes by the minute. at every hour, the monument makes time-announcements with synchronized music and motion.

PROJECT FACTS

Location: Kyoto, Japan. **Client:** Sogo & Seibu Co., Ltd. **Completion:** 2010. **Music:** Yukihiro Takahashi. **Interior design:** Tonerico Inc. and komaden corporation on engineering. **Function:** Flagship Store.

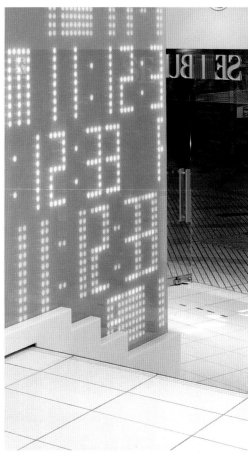

↑ | **Street view**
↓ | **Baggages' re-packing signage counter**

↑ | **Detail of pillar with LED time display**
↓ | **Sign,** handicapped access

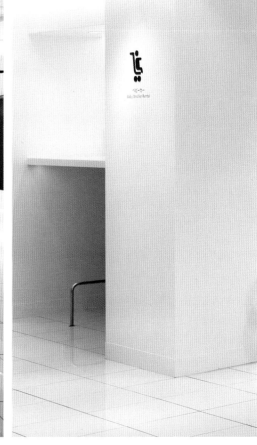

Fabio Ongarato Design

↑ | Exterior clad in shiny black circular
tiles, featuring shop sign and logo

Igloo Zoo
Melbourne

The first Igloo Zoo store, selling "super chilled yogurt", is designed as part of a complete brand experience. The glossy white epoxy floor looks as though it was poured from the yogurt machine, as does the curved banquette seating. Super graphics on the wall reference the other two flavors. A limed timber screen meanders around the store, providing enclosure and warmth while referencing both the "zoo" and "igloo".

Address: 195 Glenferrie Road, Melbourne VIC 3144, Australia. **Client:** Igloo Zoo. **Completion:** 2008.
Function: Yogurt shop.

↑ | Interior view of neon signage installed
on the window
↓ | Exterior view of neon signage

↑ | Graphics are subtly used as wallpaper
in the interior

Büro North

↖↖ | Exterior signage
↖ | Ceiling-mounted directional signage
↑ | Freestanding touch screen kiosk

Westfield Sydney
Sydney

Buro North's design solution for the wayfinding and signage system creates a dialogue between the façade designed by John Wardle Architects and the interiors designed by Wonderwall Japan. A neutral, sophisticated palette of white on white was adopted, referencing materials from the rest of the project and integrating with the interior environment seamlessly. The façade signs, directional signs and interactive kiosks are impossibly thin and delicate, featuring bright white LED illumination on minimalist white backdrops, with the text illuminated to give the required contrast ratio. Along with the wayfinding and signage package, the designers produced interpretive heritage solutions for Westfield that included embedded stainless steel site-specific quotes in the paving at major entrances and an illuminated timeline tracking the history of the site.

PROJECT FACTS

Address: 188 Pitt Street, Sydney NSW 2000, Australia. **Client:** Westfield Design and Construction. **Completion:** 2010. **Façade design:** John Wardle Architects. **Interior design:** Wonderwall Japan. **Function:** Shopping center.

↑ | **Free-standing directional sign, fourth level**
↓ | **Graphic detail of ceiling-mounted directional sign**

↑ | **Freestanding touch screen kiosk**
↓ | **Informational sign**

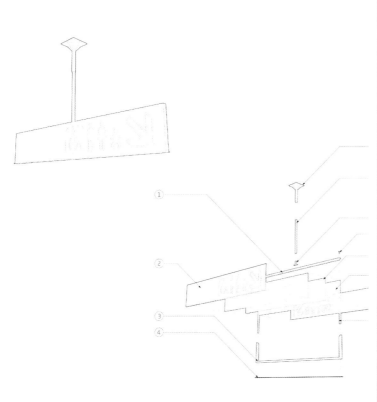

Sid Lee

↖ | Wall informational signage
↑↑ | Exterior sign
↑ | Advertising sign

Vidéotron
Montreal

Quebecor media's Videotron is a sales center for services, like mobile phone and television subscriptions. Combining a flashing LED façade, glowing glass floors and video technology; the shop's décor is based around the company's trademark black and yellow shades. From the street, passers-by can glimpse inside to see a massive staircase with a LED screen that continuously plays videos and graphics by Sid Lee and Moment Factory. The store features a graphics-oriented environment, putting content front and center.

Location: Montreal (QC), Canada. Client: Vidéotron. Completion: 2010. Function: Sales center for mobile phone and television services.

↑ | Service sign
↓ | 3D informational graphics

↑ | Interior logo sign

Redmond Schwartz
Mark Design

↑↑ | **Exterior identification sign**
↖ | **Rendering of exterior identity**
↑ | **Interior food court and MIG jet**

Loop 5
Weiterstadt

RSM Design developed a full branding, identity, and wayfinding program for this unique retail center in central Germany. The environmental graphics program was inspired by the project's location in an area known for its aeronautical history schd production within the aviation industry. The graphics created a cultural bridge from the heritage of the area to a thoroughly modern shopping experience, using many references from the different eras of flight. The specialty graphics centered around a world of aviation and its history created through specialty paving, suspended art features, wall murals, and a unique wayfinding family of signs. Even a full size historic MIG jet hangs from the ceiling of the central atrium and food court to create a one-of-a-kind community meeting place.

PROJECT FACTS

Location: Weiterstadt, Germany. **Client:** Sonae Sierra. **Completion:** 2009. **Architects:** HPP Architects. **Function:** Shopping mall.

↑ | Exterior detail of Loop 5 identity
↓ | Interior pedestrian directional signs

↓ | Wayfinding sign detail construction drawing

Frost* Design

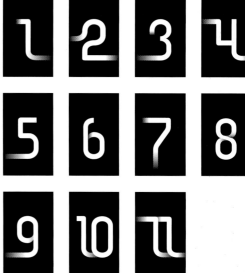

↖↖ | Building façade signage covers seven storys
↑↑ | Typography numbers
↖ | Logo and pictograms
↑ | External building identification

Molonglo Group
Canberra

Frost* Design developed an identity that references the distinctive black and white striped effect of the base building. This idea has been brought to life with huge signage on the main building façade, covering seven storys and reaching more than 26 meters high and almost as wide. The signform appears to flow in and out of the building like a ribbon. This strong visual language continues throughout the interiors of all typical floors, folding and over-lapping, using positive and negative space, and black and white contrast to create a unique and highly recognizable identity for the building.

PROJECT FACTS
Location: Canberra, Australia. Client: Molonglo Group. Completion: 2010. Architect: Architectus. Façade engineer: Arup. Function: Commercial building.

Frost* Design

↑↑ | Exterior signage
↗↗ | Identity shops' signs
↑ | Store glazed signage panel sign
↗ | Shop sign integrates lighting

Queen Victoria Building
Sydney

The new signage projects a contemporary image within the historic setting of the Queen Victoria Building – an image of internationalism and modern technology, supporting the retail strategy. Signage was placed onto existing structures as new forms; use of glazed signage panels allowed the existing structure to be exposed as much as possible. Lighting was integrated into the signage to help reduce the QVB's overall energy consumption by 42%. The signage, materials and lighting reinforce the grandeur of the building and its position as a high-end shopping destination, providing a greater sense of luxury for visitors.

PROJECT FACTS
Location: Sydney, Australia. **Client:** Ipoh. **Completion:** 2009. **Function:** Shopping mall.

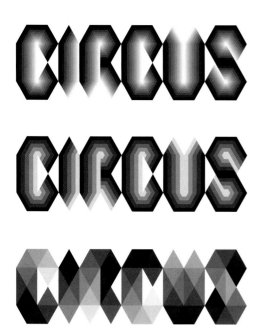

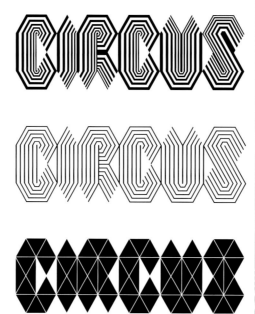

ↈↈ | **Logo based on the shape of a kaleido-
scope**
ↈ | **Typography**
↑ | **Bartabs**

Circus
London

Identity for a new club and restaurant with a burlesque theme and changing performances.
Since the club interior features many mirrored surfaces, the design of the logo is based on
the shape of a kaleidoscope. The outline shape and basic constrution of the logo always
remains the same while the inside changes depending on its application. Other influences
came from Surrealism, Art Deco, Alice in Wonderland, animals and the steps leading up to
the large table that doubles as a stage. A main feature of the interior is a three-dimensional
version of the logo built from different layers of perspex, set into a wall and illuminated
from the back in changing colors.

PROJECT FACTS

Location: London, United Kingdom. **Completion:** 2009. **Interior design:** Tom Dixon/ Design Research Studio. **Function:** Restaurant.

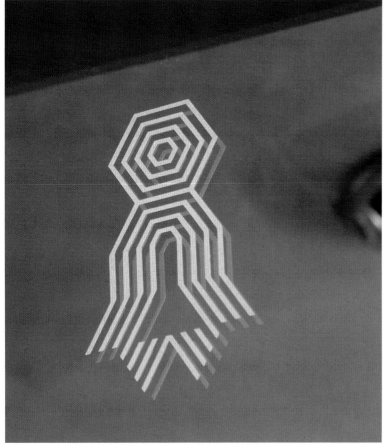

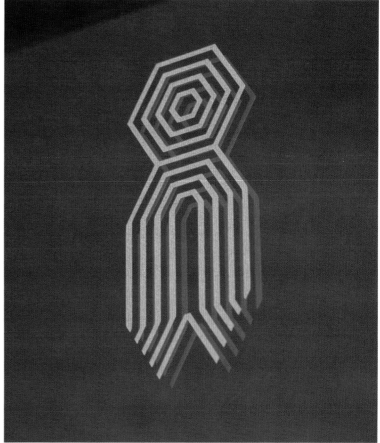

↑ | Female's restroom sign
↓ | Three-dimensional version of the logo

↑ | Male's restroom sign

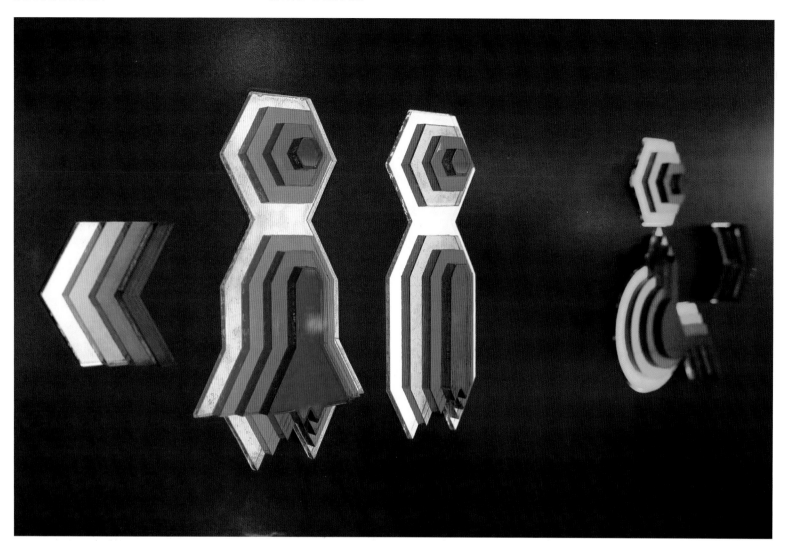

↖ | Restroom colorful signs following the logo's shape
←← | Three-dimensional blue version of the logo built from different layers of perspex
↑ | Iilluminated logo changes colors
← | Detail of logo material

↑↑ | **Exterior signage**
↖ | **Interior logo sign**
↑ | **Logo**

Paramount
London

The Paramount identity consists of a set of four graduation patterns which express an up-wards movement. Each pattern is made from one of four simple shapes (hexagon, triangle, circle and stripe) that can be found in the building or the interior, repeated 33 times (for 33 floors). Different sections of the pattern have been used for different applications. Variation was important as there were many different applications to design (brochures, stationery, menus, tapestry, signage, sliding glass screens, etc). The difficulty was to produce a design that is elegant and appealing to the members of this rather prestigious club but at the same time staying true to the raw aesthetics of the building.

Location: London, United Kingdom. **Completion:** 2009. **Interior design:** Tom Dixon/ Design Research Studio. **Function:** A members' club and event space.

PARAMOUNT

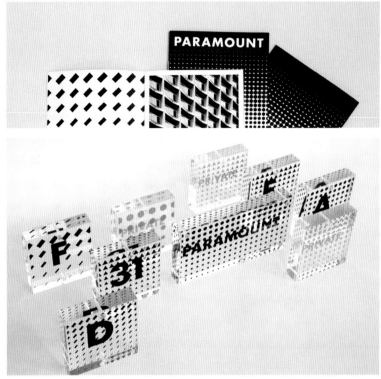

↑ | Male restroom sign
↓ | Address identification sign

↑ | Brochures
↑↑ | Informational signs printed on plexi glass

OFFICE

 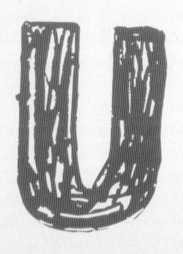 

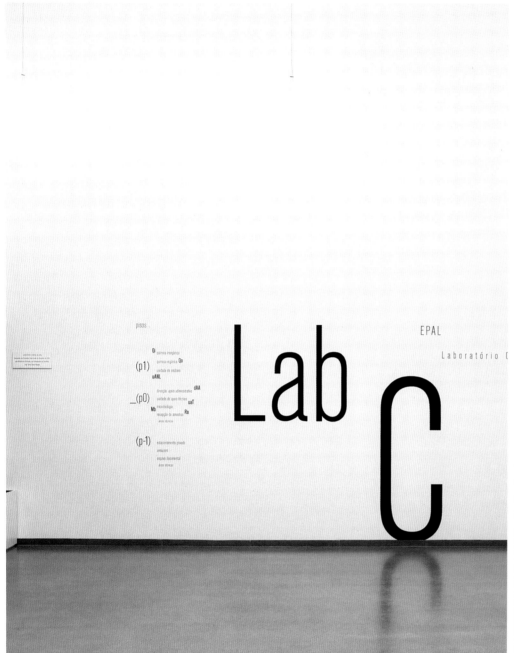

↖ | **Informational signage, main entrance**
↑↑ | **Hallway signage**
↑ | **Blue wall guiding signage**

Water Formula – EPAL
Lisbon

The graphic world of chemical equations is transferred into the wayfinding system, through contractions of names and scale differences. On the floor of the laboratories, large areas are identified by large scale applications, suitable for reading from a distance. Color fills in some areas of the building were made to simplify and organize visual space. The usage of color just on one side of the corridors and intersections is an example of this guidance support. A vibrant and bright blue was selected to liven up the interior corridors. In the parking floor, the blue wall is always on the side of the driver, simplifying the logic and perception of space.

Location: Lisbon, Portugal. **Client:** EPAL – Portuguese Water Company. **Completion:** 2010.
Architects: Gonçalo Byrne Architects. **Function:** Laboratories, offices and parking building.

↑ | Corridors in the laboratories
↓ | Examples of white and blue walls in the
basement and first floor

↑ | Chemical equations transferred into the
wayfinding system

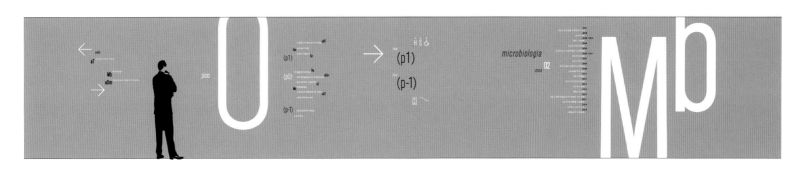

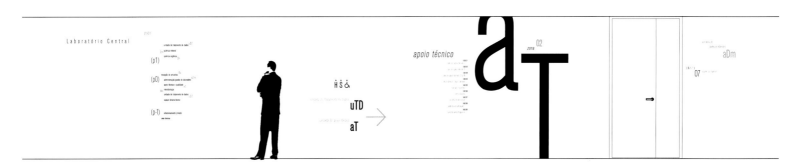

Garry Emery/ emerystudio

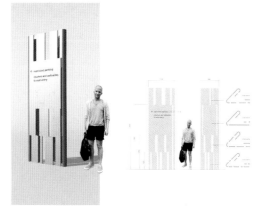

↖↖ | **Illuminated wall at entrance with narrating a story**
↑↑ | **Conceptual signage drawing**
↑ | **Informational signage**

Fairfax Media
Melbourne

A clear building addressing strategy is essential for a complex multi-level environment such as the Fairfax Media headquarters. The new building signals the transformation of a publishing company to an integrated media business. A design language was developed and extended into element of the interior architecture.

PROJECT FACTS **Location:** Melbourne, Australia. **Client:** Fairfax Media. **Completion:** 2010. **Function:** Publishing and media company.

↑ | Main entrance
↓ | Detail typography

↑ | Interior directional signage
↓ | Directional signage at street level

bauer konzept & gestaltung

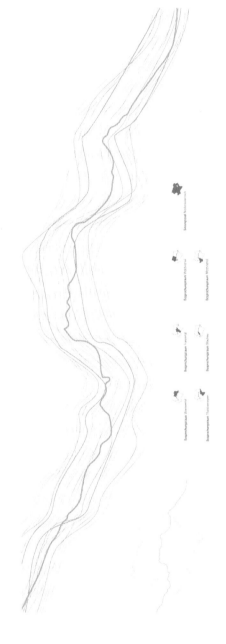

↑ I **Graphics and signs along glass surfaces-flowing through offices**

Epsilon Office
St. Pölten

Open offices, glass and transparency characterize the new building of the Lower Austrian healthcare headquarters. The interior wayfinding system in the office complex was designed to create open spaces and support basic orientation. The visual leitmotif is the permanently changing course of the Danube over the last millennia; it literally flows through the entire Epsilon office. The multi-layered line structure made of blue lacquer is used for all applications, from the floor to the door labels, as well as a principle for design elements such as pictograms. The rooms bear the names of Lower Austrian regions and are labeled with engraved natural aluminum.

PROJECT FACTS

Location: St. Pölten, Austria. **Client:** Niederösterreichische Landesklinken Holding. **Completion:** 2011.
Architect: Studio Pfaffenbichler. **Function:** Health care offices headquarters.

↑ | Signage design to mark different levels
↓ | Pictography family

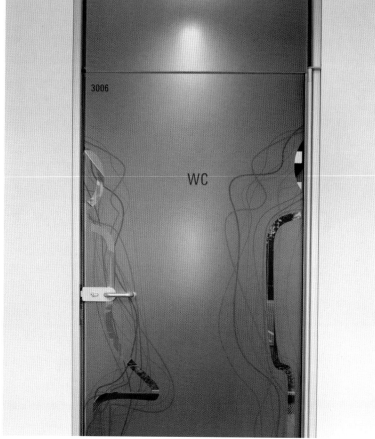

↑ | Signage design for the restrooms

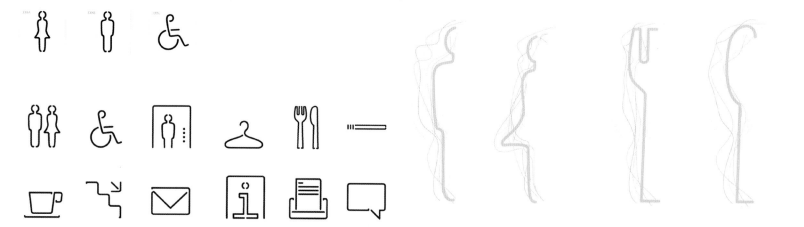

büro uebele
visuelle kommunikation

↑ | Graphic symbols cover the internal glass walls

Signage System, New Building Drägerwerk
Lübeck

The building is a glazed structure that twists and turns, ribbon-like, around courtyards and pathways. Graphic symbols cover the internal glass walls, helping to define the different moods of the various locations. The wayfinding system consists of a base motif that is modulated in six variations. At its core is a simple, grid-style pattern of rings which is different on each story. The spacing of the rings varies in two directions, creating gaps, clusters and distinctive formations. The information is incorporated within the pattern, by filling in rings to create surfaces. The codes for different rooms, levels and sections of the building are displayed within these circles.

PROJECT FACTS Location: Lübeck, Germany. **Client:** Molvina Vermietungsgesellschaft mbH und Co. Objekt Finkenstraße KG. **Completion:** 2009. **Architect:** Goetz und Hootz Architekten. **Function:** Medical and safety technology company.

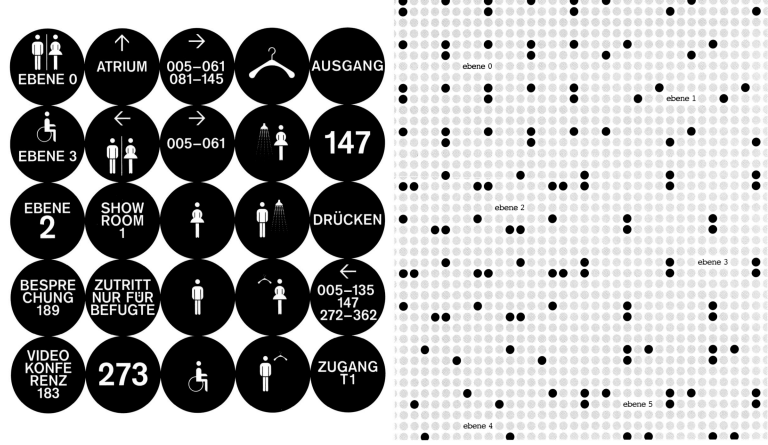

↑ | **Information structure**
↓ | **Circle on glass surface displaying room's function and number**

↑ | **Overview of ornamental annulus**

Emmanuelle Moreaux
architecture + design

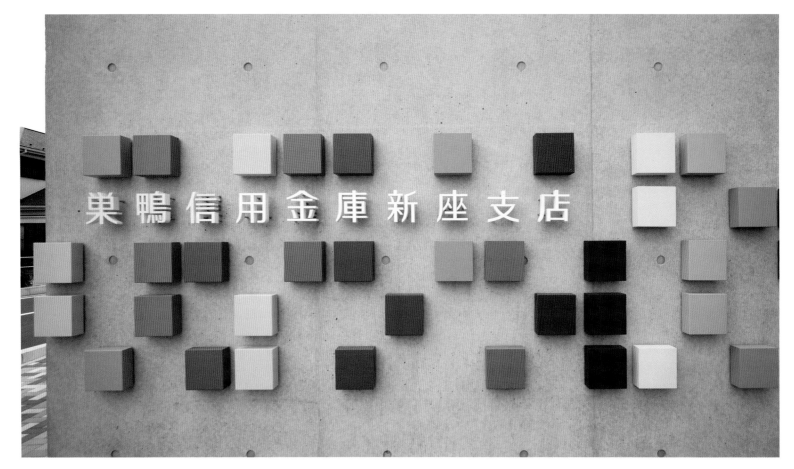

↑↑ | Logo on the façade featuring more
than 24 different square colors
↑ | Elevation

Sugamo Shinkin Bank
Niiza Branch
Saitama

This project sought to create a whole new look that refreshes the current image of this
financial institution. For their new 43rd branch, the architects redesigned not only the interior, but also Sugamo's brand image, including its façade, logo graphics, signage and brochures. The key concept revolves around squares – besides incorporating square shapes,
the building was conceived as a sort of public square where people gather. The colors of
these squares play an important role: the logo on the façade of the building features as
many as 24 colors visible from the main street, becoming a symbol for the area. These colors welcome customers as they enter the building, continuing on the inside and serving as
natural dividers between lobby, meeting space, ATM and so on.

Address: 6-1-31 Nobidome, Niiza, Saitama 352-0011, Japan. **Completion:** 2009. **Interior design, façade and sign design:** Emmanuelle Moreaux architecture + design. **Architect:** Takeo Igarashi associates × Ushigome associates. **Function:** Bank.

↑ | Front façade logo and parking lot
↓ | Service stations color-coded in pink

↓ | Tellers (green section)

←← | Detail of façade logo by night
↙ | Waiting area (orange, red, yellow section)
← | Graphical signs
↓ | Elevation (blue section)

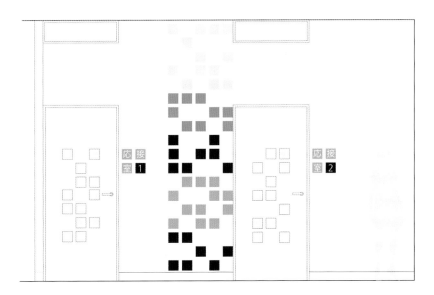

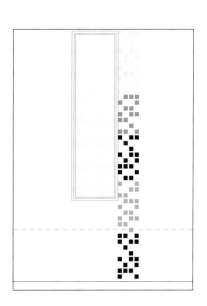

B2

C2

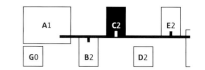

↑↑ | Pre-distorted "superflat" signage
↖ | Pre-distorted signage on "B" floor
↑ | Level "C2" signage drawing

Kreissparkasse Ludwigsburg
Ludwigsburg

The main design theme of the Kreissparkasse Ludwigsburg is "Baroque", with its architecturally mediated optical illusions; on the other hand, it is the architectural characteristic of a 140 meter-long access corridor that ties together the various new buildings. The labeling of the floors and staircases are pre-distorted by means of perspective so that from one point only they can be correctly perceived and otherwise change into free plays of form.

PROJECT FACTS
Location: Ludwigsburg, Germany. **Client:** Kreissparkasse Ludwigsburg. **Completion:** 2007. **Architect:** KBK Architekten. **Function:** Bank.

↑ | Wall with optical illusion signage
↓ | 140 meter long access corridor with pre-distorted signage

↑ | Level "E" wall painted signage

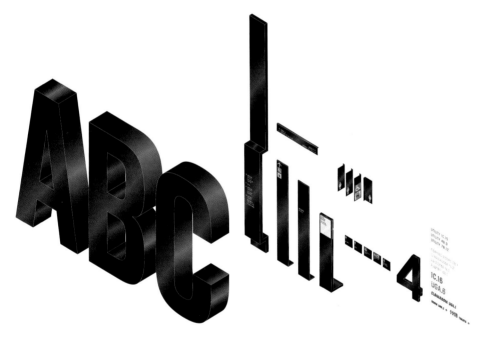

↖↖ | **Elevator wall-mounted level identification sign**
↑↑ | **Building number signage**
↖ | **Signage design detail**
↑ | **Directional signage**

ANZ Center
Melbourne

ANZ, renowned for its strong work culture, has a new head office which is home to over 6,500 staff. In collaboration with HASSELL and BLL, Fabio Ongarato Design devised a comprehensive wayfinding and environmental graphics system that matches ANZ's cultural needs and workplace values. The wayfinding system was created as an extension of the architecture. Elegant sculptural forms were directly inspired by the shifting planes that are detailed in the architecture. A diverse range of supergraphics and installations were created to simulate hub environments such as "play", "create", "grow", "move" and "click".

PROJECT FACTS

Address: 833 Collins Street, Docklands VIC 3008, Australia. **Client:** ANZ. **Completion:** 2009.
Artists: Craig McWhinney, Daniel Peterson and Maurice Lai. **Architecture and interior design:**
HASSELL and Lend Lease Design. **Signage manufacturer:** Diadem. **Floor Graphics:** Signature Flooring.
Wall Graphics: Bovis Lend Lease & Premier Graphics. **Lighting Sculpture:** JSB Lighting. **Function:** Bank.

↑ | Elevator identification signage (freestanding
backlit letterform)
↓ | Ground floor – primary directional signage

↓ | Floor level three-dimensional signage
mounted on wall

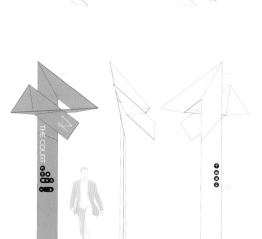

↖ | **Sculpture with company logo**
↑↑ | **Front façade signage**
↑ | **Sign scale diagram**

500 Bourke Street
Melbourne

The refurbishment of the 500 Bourke Street consisted in upgrading or replacing building services and finishes, redevelopment of the ground floor foyer and the creation of "The Court" along the Little Bourke Street and laneway façades. The Court is a boutique restaurant and retail plaza maximizing the unique outlook over the Supreme Court precinct as well as reinvigorating the city laneways on either side of the site. The integration a two-dimensional logo on a sculpture and the bright colored signage stands out in the exterior and interior.

Address: 500 Bourke Street, Melbourne VIC 3000, Australia. **Client:** ISPT. **Completion:** 2010. **Function:** National Australia Bank city headquarters.

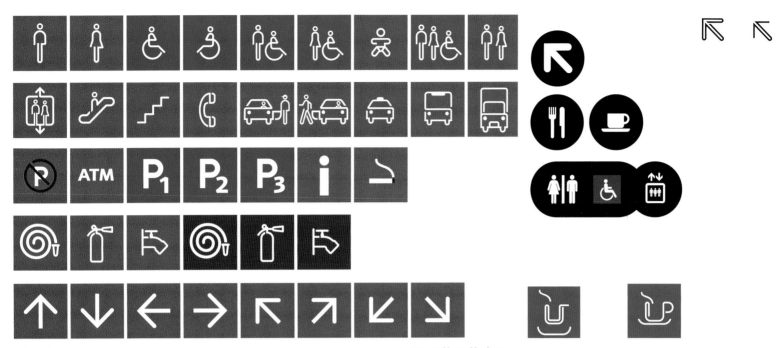

↑ | Pictograms
↓ | Signage along Bourke Street

↓ | Detail wall sign

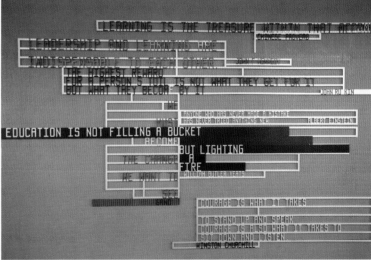

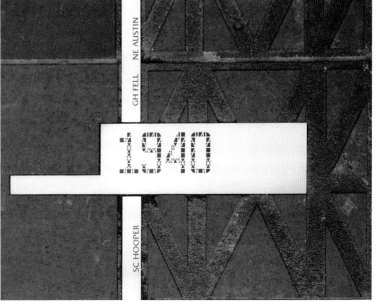

↖ | Second and third floor signage in
landing between stairs
↑ | Men's restroom door sign stretches
down onto hallway floor

Morisawa Corporate
Headquarter Building
Osaka

Morisawa is a font maker, established in 1948 as a phototypesetting maker. Through the
new corporate headquarter building, it aims to convey the importance of letters and the
philosophy of Morisawa into the future. The signage system was created with the font of
Morisawa, "Kohcho", converted into three-dimensional form, and the shadow of the letter
continues from the wall to the floor. In the landing between stairs, the shadow reaches the
ceiling. The three-dimensional form and its shadow are designed to make people aware of
the existence of letters and think about the role of letters in our society.

PROJECT FACTS Location: Osaka, Japan. **Client:** Morisawa & Company, Ltd. **Completion:** 2009. **Typeface:** Kohcho. **Function:** Font maker company.

← | Three-dimensional 9th floor signage
↙ | 5th floor signage shadow continues
from the wall to the floor
↓ | Three-dimensional 5th floor signage

↑↑ I **Logo sign**
↖ I **Glass surface sign painted in white**
↑ I **Oversized black silhouettes, used as a**
graphic sign

Congstar Office
Cologne

Besides references to the company's philosophy (young, dynamic, flexible), Congstar colors, patterns, and slogans ("Du willst es. Du kriegst es.") all enjoy a special standing. The application of black silhouettes becomes an elemental stylistic device within the holistic concept of Congstar office and lounge. Those silhouettes are dimensionally oversized, presenting various situations of telecommunications and meeting points. This graphic center of attraction supports and creates a unique Congstar atmosphere.

↑ | Graphic sign indicating the communication area
↓ | Congstar slogans sign

↑ | Relaxation area with two-dimensional signage on wall

↖ | Directional signage engraved in concrete pillar
↑↑ | Flag sign at entrance
↑ | Directional signage

Signage System Grey / G2 Group
Dusseldorf

The agency network GREY Group's new premises feature a comprehensive design and implementation for signposting, which both serves a function and is representative of the group. The design and choice of materials thus follows the visual theme of classic border markings, supplemented by a system of ceiling signs in buildings, which follow a cartographic style.

Location: Dusseldorf, Germany. **Client:** Grey Group. **Completion:** 2008. **Function:** Advertising Agency.

↑ | Ceiling in hallway with directional signs
↓ | Exterior concrete pillar with directional signs

↑ | Sign engraved in concrete pillar with integrated lighting
↓ | Conference room sign

KONFERENZRAUM 1

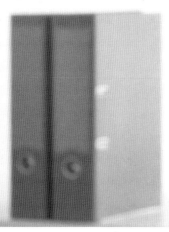

L2M3 Kommunikation
design

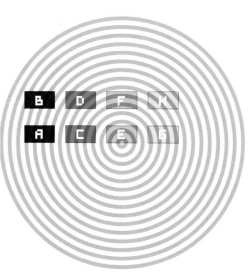

↖↖ | **Entrance with illuminated informa-
tional cube signage**
↑↑ | **Entrance informational signage**
↖ | **Hallway with directional room signage**
↑ | **Conceptual diagram**

MTZ Münchner Technologiezentrum
München

The signage system for the MTZ combines media elements with graphical, analogue elements to create a unified whole. Starting out from an assumed center point in the entrance
area, concentric circles stretch out around the building. Furthermore, illuminated, colorful
cubes at the entrance point the way to the appropriate part of the building with the aid of
animated typography. The colors stand for the various building modules. Visitors also find
the concentric circles on the ceilings in the staircase cores. The varying curve of the circles
defines the distance from the center point.

PROJECT FACTS

Address: Agnes-Pockels-Bogen 1, 80992 München, Germany. **Client:** Stadtwerke München,. **Completion:** 2009. **Architect:** h4a | Gessert + Randecker Architekten. **Function:** Technology center.

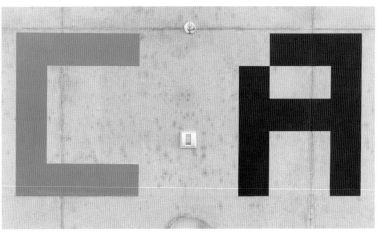

MTZ
0123456789
ABCDEFGHIJKLMNOP
QRSTUVWXYZ . - /

↑ | Illuminated, colorful cube signage
↓ | Two-dimensional wall signage

↑↑ |Two-dimensional wall informational signage
↑ | Typography

Nikolaus Schmidt Design

↑ | Lobby with informational signage on walls

Branding & Signage of the JTI headquarter
Vienna

The visual concept and typographical solution of the branding and signage for the Austria Tabak / Japan Tobacco International headquarters in Vienna are based on the company's historical and statistical data that communicate the core values of the company and its brands throughout the entire building. Based on the graphic concept, Nikolaus Schmidt Design has – in cooperation with Durig and Prenner architects – also been responsible for the interior makeover which included new flooring, furnishings and plants.

PROJECT FACTS

Location: Vienna, Austria. **Client:** Austria Tabak / Japan Tobacco International. **Completion:** 2010.
Architects: Durig and Prenner Architects. **Function:** Tobacco headquarter company.

↑ | Detail of wall graphics
↓ | Main entrance with address sign

↑ | Staircase with information on wall
surface

GSC Austria	Robert Seibezeder
GSCA	GSC Austria
GSCA/OS	Operations Services
GSCA/PS	Production Services
GSCA/OL	Operations Logistics

←←| Lobby
↙↙ | Meeting rooms with text on glass surfaces
← | Detail of floor signage
↓ | Hallway

MEMPHIS

Memphis was launched in 1896. Oriental mixtures were the high fashion at the turn of the century.

In 1969 Memphis was introduced as a filter cigarette, which is now also known as Memphis Classic and is one of the favourite brands in Austria.

The success of the product caused Austria Tabak to gradually extend the brand to a whole brand family in Austria.

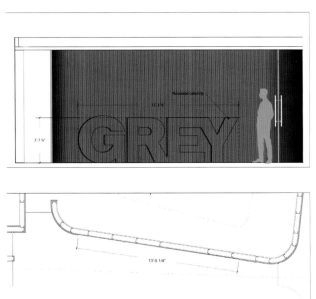

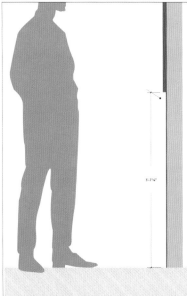

↑↑ | **Logo rendered in logo mesh**
↖ | **Elevation signage**
↑ | **The restroom graphics as seen through the courtyard**

Grey Group
New York

Paula Scher and her team at Pentagram developed an inventive program of environmental graphics for the state-of-the-art New York headquarters of Grey Group, one of the largest marketing communications companies in the world. Designed by Studios Architecture, the offices are located in a building that formerly housed several toy companies and have been designed around an open floorplan that helps promote collaboration and creative interaction among employees and the Grey agencies. Scher designed graphically playful signage that captures and promotes the creativity of the company's various divisions. The program utilizes materials used in the interior design to create a series of optical illusions that brand the agency in the space.

PROJECT FACTS

Address: 200 5th Avenue, New York (NY) 10010, USA. **Client:** Grey Group. **Completion:** 2009.
Architect: Studios Architecture. **Function:** Marketing communications company.

↖ | Painted men's restroom icon
↑ | Restrooms with superscale female icon
graphically stretches down to the hallway
← | The painted restroom icon extends
down to the hallway's floor

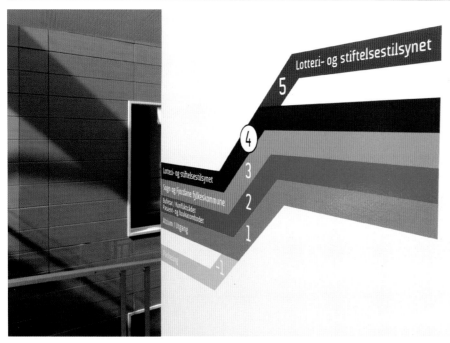

↖↖ | **Office sign**
↑↑ | **Elevator features subway signage design system**
↖ | **Informational signage indicating floor levels**
↑ | **Office glass surface sign**

Storehagen Atrium
Førde

The idea was inspired by the fact that Storehagen Atrium will be an important hub in Førde, a city with the desire to become a metropolis. Characteristic subway lines are used all through the signage system with strong colors and graphical shapes dedicated to each floor and institution. The design follows the principles of Universal design, making it easy for any user, like people with visual impairment, to find their way. The project also consisted in designing the exterior and interior signs, from directions in the public areas to the name labeling on each office door. Each of the 200 doors in the building has a unique design pattern.

Location: Førde, Norway. **Completion:** 2010. **Function:** Government building.

↑ | Glazed façade with 12 meter-high graphics
↓ | Sign indicates first floor with the braun color subway-looking line

↑ | Floor entrance sign on the fifth floor

↖ | **Leo Burnett painted from floor-to-ceiling and a sculptural Leo Burnett pencil**
↑↑ | **Exterior wall sign extends down to the floor to create a path**
↑ | **Hallway with message written on wall**

Leo Burnett Office
Singapore

The keynote of the space is a large drawing of the agencies founder, Leo Burnett, along side a scaled pencil bearing the company name. This element draws visitors into the "space to impress" a welcoming area highlighting the firms past successes. From there, the space is broken up into two more distinct areas – a place for relaxation and a place for work. Ministry of Design took inspiration for Burnett's stature as a "quintessential ad man" mixing up playful graphic with utilitarian ply wood desks.

PROJECT FACTS
Location: Singapore, Singapore. **Client:** Leo Burnett. **Completion:** 2009. **Function:** Advertising agency.

↑↑ | Logo sign at main entrance
↑ | Identification sign on glass surface
↗ | Detail sign

ADF Architects
Glasgow

ADF Architects commissioned the designers to reposition their brand in response to economic trends within the building and development sectors. The designers began by creating a solid identity and matching stationery. The new logo combines a direct typographic approach with a simple visual device – the forward slash. This symbol graphically represents the concepts of structure and support in architectural practice.

PROJECT FACTS
Location: Glasgow, Scottland, United Kingdom. **Client:** ADF Architects. **Completion:** 2010. **Function:** Architectural office.

↖↖ I Typography concept
↖ I Building exterior sign
↑↑ I A dot matrix forms letter
↑ I Story label painted on wall

Landratsamt Tübingen
Tübingen

The entrance to the district council offices already speaks an outreaching visual language addressed to the citizens: all of the municipalities belonging to the district point the way in the form of arrow symbols. The length of these arrows corresponds to the distance from the district council offices, while the width of the line corresponds to the respective population. The rest of the signage system follows this logic. Building components are labelled upside-down on the ceiling, a dot matrix forms letters, figures and pictograms. As a separate layer, the graphic design completes the function of the building and lends it a distinctive look.

PROJECT FACTS

Location: Tübingen, Germany. **Client:** Landkreis Tübingen. **Completion:** 2006. **Architect:** Auer + Weber + Assoziierte. **Function:** District council offices.

195

↑ | Story label
↓ | Supergraphic arrows painted on ceiling

↑ | Pictograms in restrooms out of a dot of matrix
↓ | Ceiling graphics
↓↓ | Supergraphic on ceiling

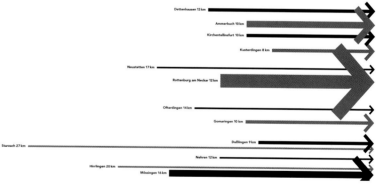

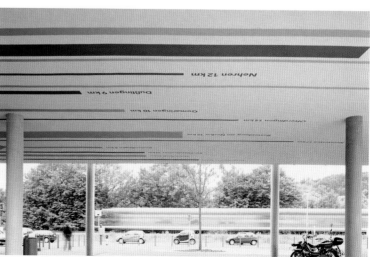

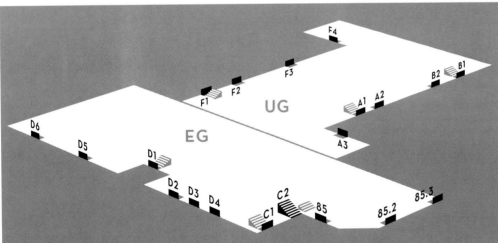

↑↑ | **Building identity sign**
↖ | **Door entrance plan**
↑ | **Building number painted on glass
surface projects out**

Aufbau Haus
Berlin

Moniteurs developed an individual orientation system, with the concept "type and material", for the Aufbau Haus at Moritzplatz. The two main tenants, "Aufbau-Verlag" and "Modulor", with its adjacent "Planets", as well as galleries, designers and photographers house the building. The signage system structures the around 19,000 square meter house. Allowing a diversity of over forty creatives, to each come to its full advantage. Cut out name lines and seemingly three-dimensional symbols give the Aufbau Haus its own identity.

↑ | Cut-out metal typed-like names
mounted on concrete wall
↓ | Typography sign detail

↓ | Informational sign in lobby

PUBLIC / TRAFFIC

büro uebele
visuelle kommunikation

↖↖ | Directional signage on bright painted wall
↑↑ | Avenir font works in counterpoint to the stark, rectangular stripes on the signs
↖ | Directional signage, number and arrows painted directly on the wall
↑ | Door sign

Trade Fair and Exhibition Center
Stuttgart

The combination of colors and lettering creates a distinctive identity for the venue and the trade fair company. The chord of colors is like a pattern, like colorful wallpaper that makes the uptake of information both pleasant and easy. The use of paired shades brings the architecture to life, the color-coding of the various destinations works at subliminal level. The colorful stripes inside lead visitors to their destination: pink leads to the conference center, green to the exits, red to the exhibition halls. The blue flag-like signs outdoors regulate the traffic. The people who will be reading them determine their height: bus and truck drivers, pedestrians and car drivers read the information from different angles.

PROJECT FACTS

Location: Stuttgart, Germany. **Client:** Projektgesellschaft Neue Messe Stuttgart. **Completion:** 2008. **Architect:** Wulf & Partner. **Product design:** ZieglerBürg Büro für Gestaltung. **Function:** Trade fair.

↑ | Hall numbers and first aid sign
↓ | Signs and pictograms

↑ | Exterior signage
↓ | Informational signage hanging from ceiling

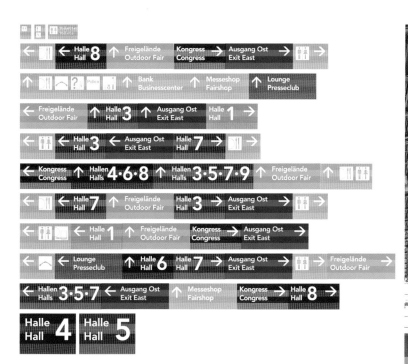

Büro North

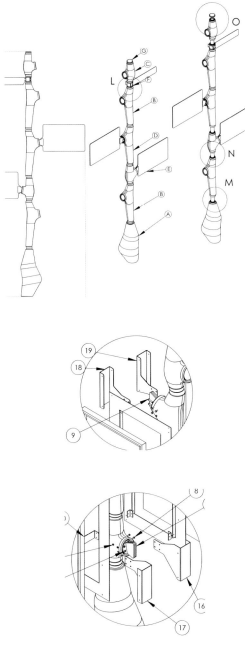

↑ | Alpine village map and information panel

Falls Creek Wayfinding and Signage
Falls Creek

The Falls Creek Alpine Resort required the development of a wayfinding system to help visitors navigate the complex ski resort. A modular system of sign types was created to provide information in a wide variety of directions to suit the complex village layout and changing seasonal functions. The designed system needed to be an environmentally conscious solution to match the resort's claim as the first alpine-based organization to be benchmarked by Green Globe 21: the international certification program for sustainable tourism.

PROJECT FACTS

Location: Falls Creek, Victoria, Australia. **Client:** Falls Creek Resort Management. **Completion:** 2010.
Function: Wayfinding and signage design for ski resort.

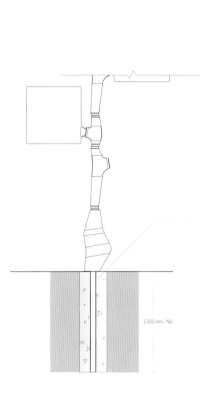

↑ | **Detail of footing diagram**

↑ | **Directional sign**
↓ | **Directional sign by road side**

großgestalten
kommunikationsdesign

↖ | **Vivid orange, large typography sign**
↑ | **Color-coded informational sign**

Rheinauhafen
Cologne

The orientation system guides people through the newly designed harbor area in Cologne which combines listed buildings with contemporary architecture. With the choice of rust-red Corten steel, glass, and colored light strips, the system incorporates materials found in the area's buildings, and thus harmoniously adapts to the environment. Colors, numbers, names, and steles serving as information carrier provide easy orientation in the area subdivided into eight spaces. Strong colors give the underground parking lot a friendly character.

PROJECT FACTS

Location: Colgne, Germany. **Client:** Häfen und Güterverkehr Köln AG, Cologne. **Completion:** 2009.
Function: Residential and parking.

↑ | **Parking garage directional signage**
↓ | **Identity signage** on glazed façade

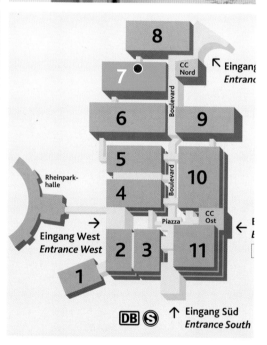

↖ | Exterior identity sign
↑↑ | Hall number and site plan sign
mounted over door entry
↖ | Cube sign with hall number and
directional signs
↑ | Floor plan

Cologne Trade Fair Center
Cologne

The design task was a highly complex one – because of the differences between the individual buildings and building dimensions, the way the exhibition center is interlocked into its dense urban context and the need to integrate the newly built extension on the north side. The new wayfinding and information system is based on a strong concept; it is functional and supports a unified visual identity, taking into account the existing CI guidelines of the trade-fair company. Good orientation around the site is ensured by site plans, signage, and zone identification and, during events, by the halls' plans on which the individual stands and companies are marked.

Location: Cologne, Germany. **Completion:** 2009. **Architects:** W & P Architekten Ingenieure, KSP Engel und Zimmermann Architekten, sic gmbH Generalplaner architekten ingenieure. **Function:** Trade fair.

↑ | Green balloon signs indicate the aisles with the individual trade fair stands
↓ | Registration numbers on a white strip, run along wall behind the counters

↑ | Directional signage suspended from ceiling structure in lobby area

ma:design

↖↖ | Lockers's assigned number
↖ | Letter section sign
↑ | Logo signage painted on top of the chimney

eFFeMMe23 Library
La Fornace
Ancona

Ma:design created a corporate identity and signage system that transformed the library in a community center. The logo, white painted on the top of the chimney, dominates both the town of Moie and the surrounding valleys. The whole communication is based on the use of the phonetic alphabet, a hybrid form of expression, in which reading and writing coincide and overlap. It characterizes all the communicative supports and it is also used on the perimeter windows, marking the elliptical path of the building.

Address: Via Fornace, 23, Moie di Maiolati Spontini, 60030 Ancona, Italy. **Client:** City of Maiolati Spontini. **Completion:** 2010. **Function:** Library.

↑ | Entrance window signage stickers, indicating the library opening hours
↓ | Toilet pictograms, all based on the letter "Y"

↓ | Lockers with three-dimensional numbers

Naoki Terada/ Terada Design Architects

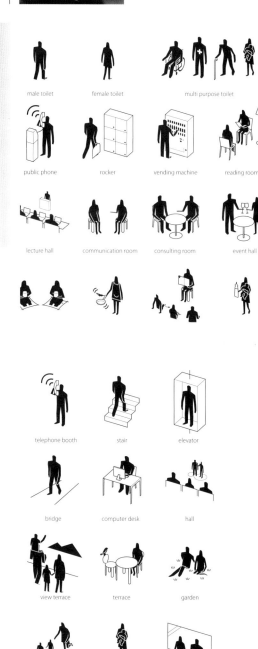

↖ | **Informational signage, restroom**
↑ | **Pictograms**

Shiojiri City Communication Center Library

Nagano

This multi-complex facility for a community center housing a library, a child care support center and a convention hall was seeking an overall graphic identity; Naoki Terada/ Terada Design Architects with the use of pictograms placed within the facility, created fragments or scenes of our everyday life. The pictogram of the public phone is not the "phone" itself, but the "person speaking on the phone". The pictogram of the staircase is not just the "stairs", but the "people going up and down the stairs".

Location: Nagano, Japan. **Client:** Shiojiri City. **Completion:** 2010. **Architect:** Jun Yanagisawa. **Function:** Communication center library.

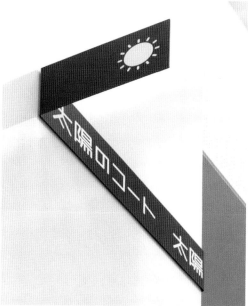

↖ | Bicycle parking signage
↑↑ | Telephone, vending machine, lockers signage
↑ | Sign indicating courtyard direction
← | Terrace signage on glass surface

Büro für Gestaltung
Wangler & Abele

↖ | Large scale directional signage and site plan in lobby area
↑ | Gate number sign over door entry way

Hamburg Trade Fair Center
Hamburg

The idea of "communication in space" takes into account the zoning of the areas, spaces, roads and paths within the center, as well as lines of sight and fields of view. Just a few basic elements – in terms of format, typography and pictograms – ensure formal consistency and characterize the visual design. A plan of the center, a recurring element to support orientation, is presented in a reduced form, and is easy to understand. Sign dimensions are oriented to the module dimensions used in the architectural design, and to the distances from which the users should be able to see them. Large scale lettering on buildings and posts – for information or advertising related to the individual event – were also developed out of the overall design concept. This also applies to the supplementary objects designed for the public spaces.

Location: Hamburg, Germany. **Completion:** 2008. **Architects:** Ingenhoven Architects. **Function:** Trade fair.

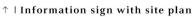

↑ | Information sign with site plan
↓ | Hall number sign

↑ | Large scale directional and informational hall sign
↓↓ | Section

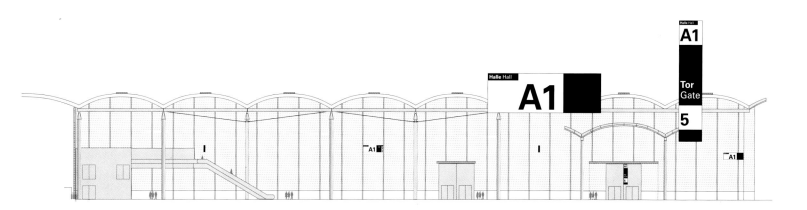

Mike and Maaike

↖ | Exit wallpaper sign on ceiling, above stairs
↑↑ | Blue and white restroom's wallpaper sign
↖ | Gray and white restroom's wallpaper sign
↑ | Floor level wallpaper sign

Wayfinder Wallpaper
Various

"Wayfinder wallpaper" is a line of wallpaper designed to serve a functional purpose within the context of architecture, while wallpapers are typically decorative, here they are embedded with symbols which serve as a wayfinding system for visitors. Symbols are typically functional. The combination of the two creates new possibilities for architects, interior designers and space planners.

PROJECT FACTS
Completion: 2010. **Manufactured:** Rollout. **Function:** Multiple.

Frost* Design

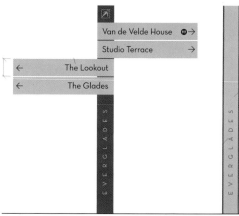

↑↑ | Construction detail of sign
↗↗ | Signage elevation drawing
↑ | Informational sign with black and white photos from the Everglades
↗ | Directional signage

Everglades
Leura, Blue Mountains

Frost* Design developed a signage and wayfinding system, ensuring the design was sympathetic to landscape and its existing features. The "leaf" in the National Trust brand inspired the signage color system of pale green with a burst of bright green on the side profile. The signage system was used to strengthen the brand and communicate to visitors that the site was a part of a collection of significant national sites. A selection of beautiful black and white photographs from the Everglades archives were chosen for the interpretive graphics to contextualize the history of the grounds. The wayfinding signage and interpretive graphics have assisted in re-establishing Everglades as a landmark destination for locals and tourists alike.

PROJECT FACTS

Address: Leura, Blue Mountains, Australia. **Client:** National Trust of Australia. **Completion:** 2011. **Construction:** Consolidated Graphics. **Function:** Interpretive signage and mapping for heritage house and garden.

Frost* Design

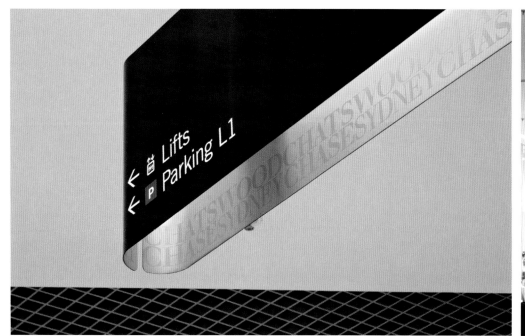

↖↖ | Suspended directional signage
↑↑ | Suspended wayfinding signage
↖ | Large scale floor level signage in parking garage
↑ | Elevation typical parking garage entry to lift lobby, Levels G and 1

Chatswood Chase Sydney
Sydney

The new holistic signage scheme in the upgraged shopping center covered each of the four shopping levels, and included major external and internal identification, directional and operational signage. The new branding inspired a classic black and white palette for the signage, working to establish a sense of place integrated with the interior scheme. The center's 1950s Artichoke lights hanging in the atrium were referenced in the design of the suspended wayfinding signage. Large scale painted supergraphics provide clear wayfinding messages throughout the carpark.

Location: Sydney, Australia. **Client:** Colonial First State. **Completion:** 2009. **Function:** Shopping mall wayfinding and parking garage.

↑ | Large scale painted supergraphics in parking garage
↓ | Elevation B2 parking garage wall

↙↙ | Elevation, suspended directional sign to parking garage level B1 and detail of typical letter
↓↓ | Valet parking sign painted from floor-to-ceiling

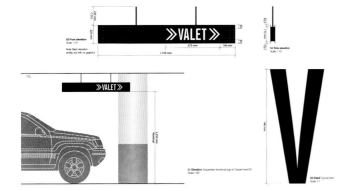

Latitude Group

↖↖ | Entry colorful sign
↑↑ | Large scale colorful signage
↖ | "Hello" sign with overlaying colors

QV Melbourne Parking Garage Wayfinding
Melbourne

A series of large scale directional and environmental graphics were added to the QV Melbourne Parking Garage, one of the cleanest parking lots in the city which required a wayfinding system. Each typographic piece was individually hand painted on site overlaying the colors to produce a multiplied effect onto the brickwork. Each word was designed to fit into the exacting locations available on site providing visibility from the street as well as a welcomed use of color on the underground levels.

PROJECT FACTS
Location: Melbourne, Australia. **Completion:** 2010. **Function:** Parking garage.

219

↑ | **Floor-to-ceiling "down" sign**
↓ | **Exit sign extends between two ventilation**
units, floor to ceiling.

BrandCulture
Communications

↑ | **Loading zone overhead signage**

World Square Parking Garage
Sydney

World Square Parking Garage is a simple parking lot easy to navigate. Located in the heart of Sydney's CBD, the World Square Parking Garage is an amalgamation of several parking garages situated under new developments that make-up the largest multi-functional complex in Australia. Covering an entire city block and bordered by four of Sydney's busiest streets in the CBD, it is home to a retail center, residential block and a hotel. The wayfinding principles consist of cognitive mapping and circulatory navigation combined with an integrated and intuitive design for the best outcome.

Location: Sydney, Australia. **Client:** Brookfield Multiplex. **Completion:** 2007. **Graphic designer:** Bobby Rakich. **Function:** Parking garage.

↑ | Parking signage wrapped around exterior column
↓ | Parking level 3 and public elevators' signage

↑ | Large scale painted floor section

← ← | Overhead parking pedestrian entrance sign
← ← | Parking level 3
↙ ↙ | Directional painted wall signage
← | Graphic and typographic "fire exit" sign
↓ | Delineated driveway

Teresa Sapey Estudio
de Arquitectura

↑ | **Hand as a directional sign**

Hotel Puerta America Parking
Madrid

Not only does the poem *Liberté* take up the entire façade of the Hotel Puerta America, but it was also a great source of inspiration for the architect Teresa Sapey, who designed the two-story underground parking lot. Her idea, based on graphics and color, was to add emotions in a space that is usually considered as dark and boring. The architect picked a number of words from the poem and rendered graphic symbols by mixing them. Being imprinted on the bright and color-saturated walls, these symbols lead guests through the garage and refer them to the idea of freedom which the hotel is based on.

Address: Calle del Corazón de María 10, 28002 Madrid, Spain. **Client:** Silken Hotels. **Completion:** 2005. **Function:** Parking garage.

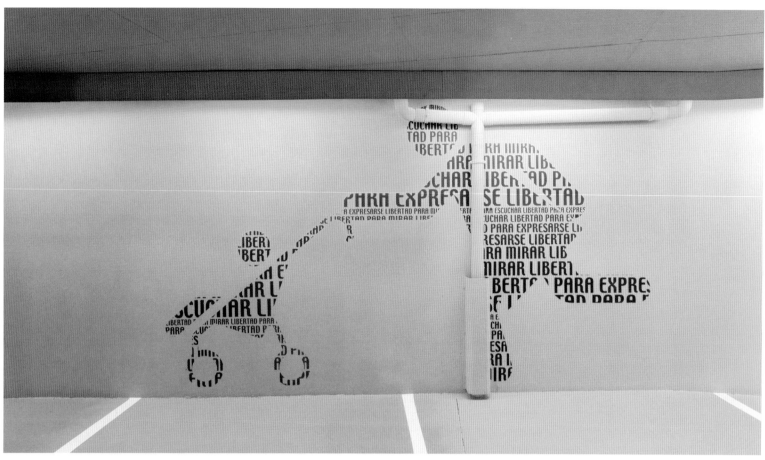

↑ | **Family parking spot**
↓ | **Parking spots close to the exit way**

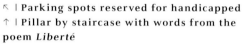
↖ | Parking spots reserved for handicapped
↑ | Pillar by staircase with words from the
poem *Liberté*
← | Reindeer rendered with words

← | Front view of hand as a directional sign
↓ | Parking spots indicating exit (salida)
way on wall
↓↓ | Elevations

Garry Emery/ emerystudio

⤡⤡ | "IN" sign painted on the wall and
stretching out to the floor
↑↑ | Bycicle parking
⤡ | "DOWN" sign falling from the wall

Eureka Tower Parking Garage
Melbourne

Inspired by the work of Swiss artist Felice Varini whose perspective-defying installations
look a lot like giant vector art superimposed on buildings or interior architectural spaces,
emerystudio designed colorful forms that are both two- and three-dimensional. Using a
projector technique for positioning, the design team painted key words and directions
directly on the garage walls and floors. From different viewpoints, the supersized letterforms can be perceived as either abstract distortions or directional information. Using an
anamorphic approach wherein the images seem distorted until the viewer's vantage point
is perfect, the words "In," "OUT," "UP, " and "DOWN" snap into alignment to convey information at key decision-making points along the way. For drivers, the result is more engag-
ing than the typical boring journey through a colorless cement cavern.

PROJECT FACTS Location: Melbourne, Australia. **Client:** Eureka Tower. **Completion:** 2006. **Function:** Parking garage.

229

↑ | Distorted sign "UP"
↓ | Slanted "OUT" sign painted on wall

↑ | "DOWN" sign appears to be melting
down the walls

P-06 Atelier

↑ | Onomatopoeic intervention under the bridge

Bikeway
Lisbon

The bikeway lane runs along the river Tagus, and with its 7362 meters it crosses different urban spaces each one demanding different solutions. The goal was to define a new urban environment beyond the bikeway, in order to improve the riverbank Belém, , an urban district of Lisbon. The selection of compatible and existing materials was considered in order to make clear the readability and use of the new system. The plane tells a story, guides the users and seduce them along this route. The route reveals touristic, cultural and natural points of interest, as well as, useful signage for transports, stops or break points. Aside from clearly evident pictograms, particular stylistic features have been incorporated, such as Alberto Caeiro's poem in large scale letters or onomatopoeic sounds under a bridge.

PROJECT FACTS

Address: Belém – Cais do Sodré, Lisbon, Portugal. **Client:** APL – Lisbon Seaport, EDP – Portugal Energy and Lisbon City Hall. **Completion:** 2009. **Landscape Architecture:** Global Arquitectura Paisagista/ João Gomes da Silva. **Function:** Bikeway.

↑ | Poems on the warehouses
↓ | Onomatopoeic intervention under the bridge

↑ | Poem over the dock pier
↓↓ | Pictography

↑ | The end or beginning of the path
↓ | Conceptual drawings

↑ | Street signage indicating the kilometers

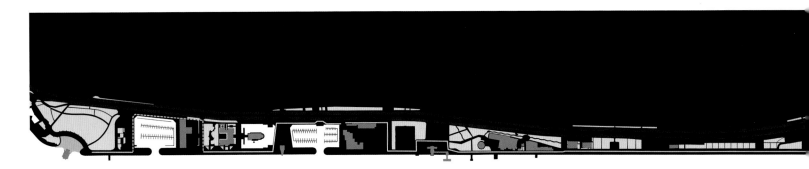

←← | Warehouses with bycicle pictogram

O TEJO TEM GRANDES NAVIOS E NAVEGA NELE AINDA, · · · · · · PARA AQUELES QUE VÊEM EM TUDO O QUE LÁ NÃO ESTÁ, · · · · · A MEMÓRIA DAS NAUS.

Teresa Sapey Estudio
de Arquitectura

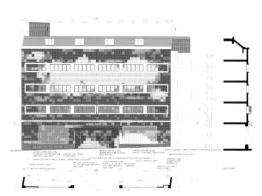

↑↑ | **Entrance to parking garage**
↖ | **Floor signage painted in white**
↑ | **Elevation**

Parking Farmacia
Madrid

This vertical parking garage, located in a building with four floors, appears to connect from the ground to heaven; the walls seem to be pixelated when going up the ramp which connects the different levels. The color blue, white sky and clouds are reproduced in the bathrooms with ceramic tiles.

↑ | White painted number indicating floor
level (4)
↓ | Detail of pixelated wall

↓ | Floor sign

Paula Scher/ Pentagram

↑ | **Signage as backseat driver: typography throughout the building directs drivers**

Parking at 13–17 East 54th Street
New York

The upgrade of this seven-story parking garage consisted of installing a new program of environmental graphics. Paula Scher's graphic concept acts as a kind of backseat driver throughout the garage, imparting information to customers via large scale typography and ensuring drivers would never forget where they parked their cars. Set in Verlag, the typographic pileup includes instructions for drivers — "Slow and steady wins the race," "Don't stop here, continue," and supergraphics identifying parking levels and elevators. The façade signage is rendered in elegant neon.

Address: 13-17 East 54th Street, New York (NY) 10022, USA. **Client:** Cohen Bros. Realty. **Completion:** 2010. **Typeface:** Verlag. **Function:** Parking garage.

↑ | Large graphics for easier direction
↓ | Informational signage installed at the parking garage's entrance

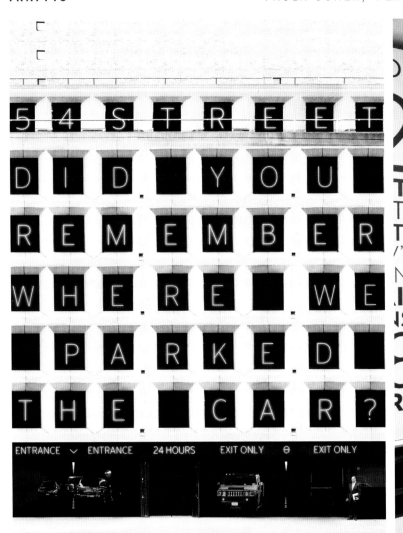

↖ | Façade signage
↑ | Informational signage at entrance
← | Signage precaution

← | Neon signage installed on the exterior of the garage
↓ | Supergraphics are installed on the elevator doors

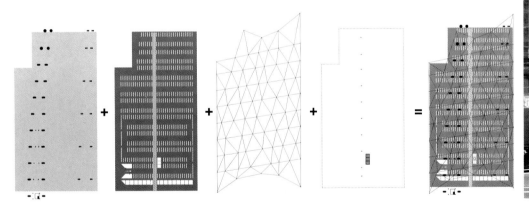

↖↖ | **Informational sign hanging from "web"**
↖ | **Concept drawing**
↑↑ | **Signing and art in "web"**
↑ | **Road directional signs**

P+R Sloterdijk
Amsterdam

This project reforms the parking at the Sloterdijk Station from wasteland to a clear part of the city. The "Piarcoplein" was a leftover space between offices and railways. To create a clear space, the architects used three main elements: huge stripping in the pavement that changes normal use to comic book acts, lighting elements and signing and artwork that has been hung into a web of wires and a transparent porters' lodge. The height of the glazed porters' lodge is increased by photographic artworks by Thomas Elshuis.

PROJECT FACTS

Location: Piarcoplein, Amsterdam Sloterdijk, The Netherlands. **Client:** City Of Amsterdam (DIVV). **Completion:** 2005. **Function:** Public parking.

↑↑ | Exit sign (Ausfahrt) and service sign
↑ | Crash barriers with large black letters
↗ | Double crash barriers

Signage System
Car Dealer Pappas
Salzburg

This dealership is a drive-through sculpture, so the design of the signage system for vehicles responds by providing a guided tour. Destinations appear in large black letters on white crash barriers: car wash, car park, service, and sales. The familiar form of the crash barrier guides visitors to their goal. The color scheme of the signage system – black and white – fits discreetly with the colorful world of the brand and the architecture.

PROJECT FACTS
Location: Salzburg, Austria. **Client:** Pappas Salzburg. **Completion:** 2006. **Building architect:** kadawittfeldarchitektur. **Function:** Car dealer.

Teresa Sapey Estudio
de Arquitectura

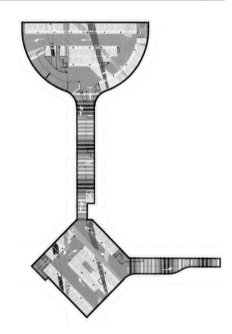

↖↖ | Parking spots reserved for electrical cars
↖ | First basement level, parking spots
↑↑ |First level ground arrow
↑ | Floor plan, first level

Plaza Cánovas de Castillo
Valencia

The parking lot Plaza Cánovas in Valencia fully embraces the theater-like creations of the designer Teresa Sapey: the four parking levels are marked with different colors that recall four possible routes for visiting the city, four canvases on which life takes place in Valencia. The green for parks and gardens, blue for the sea and the port, the yellow for crowded places like markets and the red for cultural sites, museums and churches. It is also an ecological parking lot, from the materials used to the recharging electrical cars parking spots; the concept behind this project is to persuade visitors to leave the car in Valencia and explore the city by foot, drifting from its various internal and emotional paths.

PROJECT FACTS
Location: Valencia, Spain. Completion: 2009. Function: Parking garage.

↑ | **Digital informational screens**
↗↗ | **Interior signage**
↗ | **Informational signage**

JetBlue Airways T5 at JFK
Queens (NY)

Rockwell Group worked with JetBlue to re-think the airline's brand concept and to re-imagine the T5 marketplace – a triangular retail and dining area where all three concourses will meet. JetBlue believed that the marketplace was the one area in its new terminal where it could fully exhibit its "JetBlue-ness." In response, Rockwell Group expanded JetBlue's brand concept by equating "JetBlue-ness" with "New York-ness" and created a marketplace interior concept that is bold, celebratory and affirmatively New York.

PROJECT FACTS
Address: John F. Kennedy International Airport, Queens (NY), USA. **Client:** JetBlue Airways. **Completion:** 2008. **Architect and interior designer:** Gensler. **Function:** Retail marketplace and restaurant venues.

Zup Associati Design

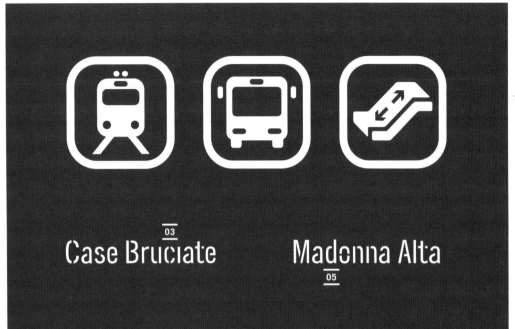

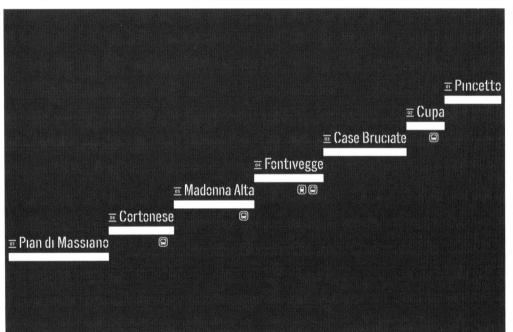

↖↖ | **Pictograms and typography**
↖ | **Graphic drawing of the metro line map**
↑↑ | **"Madonna Alta" station sign**
↑ | **"Fontivegge" metro line map** painted on wall

Minimetrò Signage
Perugia

The Minimetrò is a city's light transit system that consists of only one line. It is connected from Perugia's historic center to an ample parking area. Each of the seven Minimetrò stations was architecturally designed by Atelier Jean Nouvel. The signage project developed by Zup Associati consists of the conception of an original graphic system to identify each station, metro line maps, identification of the directional signage and the design of informational, security, hazard and prohibition pictograms.

PROJECT FACTS

Location: Perugia, Italy. **Client:** Minimetrò spa. **Completion:** 2009. **Architect:** Ateliers Jean Nouvel.
Function: Mini railway stations.

↑↑ | **"Cortonese" station**
↑ | **Elevator pictogram**
↓ | **"Fontivegge" station**

↑ | **Prohibition and informational pictograms**
↓ | **Security, hazard and prohibition pictograms**
↙↙ | **"Pian di Massimo" station**

↖ | Identity signage
↑↑ | Lightened building sign panels
↑ | Ground signage

Zeche Zollverein
Essen

The challenge of the wayfinding is to answer the needs of 500,000 visitors a year while at the same time cope with the strict regulations of the monument conservation. The design intention is to guide with minimal yet distinctive clues rather than confusing by installing a forest of signs. The keynote is: silent in terms of quantity and loud in terms of quality. It introduces a great variety of tools such as personnel, three-dimensional iron miniature models, ground markings, lightened panels as well as printed media in a combination of low-tech (cast iron, milling) and high-tech (LEDs, anodizing printing) methods.

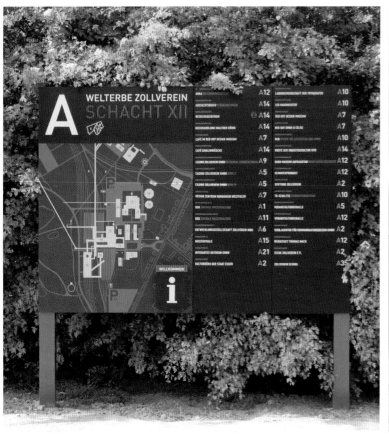

↑ | Tenants' panel
↓ | Three-dimensional miniature model

↑ | Day and night time view to hall sign
↓ | Information box and map detail
↓↓ | Elements of the wayfinding system

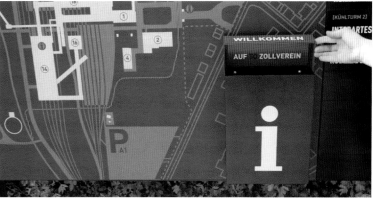

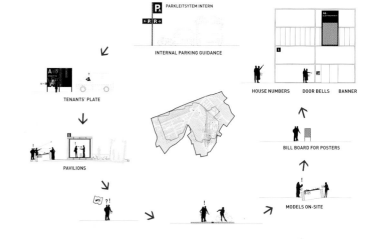

Index

Design

De

gners' Index

2. stock süd netthoevel & gaberthüel

Freiburgstrasse 54
2501 Biel (Switzerland)
T +41.32.3422505
ng@secondfloorsouth.com
www.secondfloorsouth.com

Akira Yoneda/ Architecton

1-7-16-612 Honcho
Shibuy-ku, Tokyo 151-0071 (Japan)
T +81.3.33740846
F +81.3.53652216
a-tecton@pj8.so-net.ne.jp

bauer konzept & gestaltung

Weyringergasse 36/1
1040 Vienna (Austria)
T +43.1.50448180
F +43.1.504481811
office@erwinbauer.com
www.erwinbauer.com

BOSCO

San Cristóbal 3, bajo
Valencia (Spain)
T +34.963.916638
bosco@boscographic.com
www.boscographic.com
www.boscographicblog.com

BrandCulture Communications

Suite 202, 19a Boundary Street
Rushcutters Bay, NSW 2011
Australia
T +61.2.82527522
F +61.2.82527521
info@brandculture.com.au
www.brandculture.com.au

Büro North

L1/35 LIttle Bourke Street
Melbourne 3000 (Australia)
T +61.3.96543259
F + 61.3.94459042
info@buronorth.com
www.buronorth.com

büro uebele visuelle kommunikation

Heusteigstraße 94a
70180 Stuttgart (Germany)
T +49.711.3417020
F +49.711.34170230
info@uebele.com
www.uebele.com

BWM Architekten und Partner

Margaretenplatz 4/L1
1050 Vienna (Austria)
T +43.1.2059070
F +43.1.205907020
office: office@bwm.at
bwm.at

Mary Choueiter

176 Irving Avenue, Apt #2L
Brooklyn, NY 11237 (USA)
T +1.401.4642530
mchoueiter@gmail.com
www.marychoueiter.net

compactlab creative consulting

Chemin des Poteaux 4
1213 Geneva (Switzerland)
T +41.22.3006330
F +41.22.3006331
lab@compactlab.com
www.compactlab.com

Garry Emery/ emerystudio

80 Market Street
SouthBank, VIC 3006 (Australia)
T + 61.3.96993822
F *61.3.9690.7371
info@emerystudiostudio.com
www.emerystudio.com

F1RSTDESIGN

Wilhelm-Mauser-Strasse 49c
50827 Cologne (Germany)
T: +49,221.98747710
hello@f1rstdesign.com
www.f1rstdesign.com

FBA.

Avenida Emidio Navarro 91 r/c
3000-151 Coimbra (Portugal)
T +351.239406176
F +351.239406177
info@fba.pt
www.fba.pt

→ **130**

Frost* Design

Level 1, 15 Foster Street
Surry Hills, NSW 2010 (Australia)
T +61.2.92804233
F +61.2.92804266
info@frostdesign.com.au
www.frostdesign.com.au

→ **54, 126, 148, 149, 215, 216**

Gabor Palotai Design

Västerlänggatan 56
111 29 Stockholm (Sweden)
T +46.8.248818
design@gaborpalotai.com
www.gaborpalotai.com

→ **134**

Gourdin & Müller

Fichtestraße 7
04275 Leipzig (Germany)
T +49.341.3019115
F +49.341.2319441

Barmbeker Straße 148
22299 Hamburg (Germany)
T +49.40.18050305
F +49.4018050306
info@gourdin-mueller.de
www.gourdin-mueller.de

→ **108, 136**

Graphical House

53 King Street
Glasgow, G1 5RA, Scottland (United Kingdom)
T +44.141.5535860
www.graphicalhouse.co.uk
studio@graphicalhouse.co.uk

→ **193**

großgestalten kommunikationsdesign

Vondelstraße 29–31
50677 Cologne (Germany)
T +49.221.2106120
F +49.221.2106125
info@grossgestalten.de
www.grossgestalten.de

→ **204**

Gruppe Gut

Via Cappuccini 8/15, 39100 Bolzano (Italy)
T +39.471.981700
F +39.471.981701
info@gruppegut.it
www.gruppegut.it

→ **52**

Günter Hermann Architekten

Sophienstraße 17
70178 Stuttgart (Germany)
T +49.711.607740
F +49.711.6077444
info@gharchitekten.de
www.gharchitekten.de

→ **60**

Henkelhiedl

Urbanstrasse 116
10967 Berlin (Germany)
T + 49.30.69568976
F +49.30.69568977
b@henkelhiedl.com
www.henkelhiedl.com

→ **102**

Hiromura Design Office

MAK Flat 6F, 6-11-8 Minami-Aoyama, Minato-ku
Tokyo 107 0062 (Japan)
T +81.3.3409.5546
F +81.3.3409.5572
info@hiromuradesign.com
www.hiromuradesign.com

→ **122, 132, 138, 176**

Rowin Petersma/ Inbo

Weesperstraat 3
1000 AZ Amsterdam (The Netherlands)
T +31.20.4212422
F +31.20.4212507
rowin.petersma@inbo.com
www.rowinpetersma.nl

→ **240**

JangledNerves

Hallstrasse 25
70376 Stuttgart (Germany)
T +49.711.5503750
F +49.711.55037522
info@janglednerves.com
www.janglednerves.de

→ **23**

KW43 BRANDDESIGN

Platz der Ideen 2
40476 Düsseldorf (Germany)
T +49.211.5577830
F +49.211.55778333
contact@kw43.de

→ **180**

Keggenhoff I Partner

Karlstraße 10
59755 Arnsberg-Neheim (Germany)
T +49.29.329028660
F +49.29.329028666
welcome@keggenhoff.de
www.keggenhoff.de

→ **178**

Jens Könen, Kristin Stratmann

info@jenskoenen.com
www.jenskoenen.com

→ **82**

L2M3 Kommunikationsdesign

Hoelderlinstrasse 57
70193 Stuttgart (Germany)
T + 49.711.99339160
F + 49.711.99339170
info@L2M3.com
www.l2m3.com

→ **28, 170, 182, 194**

Latitude Group

4C Cecil Place
Prahram Melbourne 3181 (Australia)
T +61.3.95295299
F +61.3.95293299
info@latitudegroup.com.au
www.latitudegroup.com.au

→ **218**

ma:design

Viale della Vittoria, 88 - 61121 Pesaro (PU) Italy
T +39.0721.371097
F +39.0721.67956
info@madesign.it
www.madesign.it

→ **30, 208**

Mike and Maaike

2459 Lombard Street
San Francisco, CA 94123 (USA)
info@mikeandmaaike.com
www.mikeandmaaike.com

→ **214**

Mind Design

Unit 33A, Regents Studios
8 Andrews Road, London E8 4QN (United Kingdom)
T +44.20.72542114
info@minddesign.co.uk
www.minddesign.co.uk

→ **106, 118, 150, 154**

Ministry of Design

20 Cross Street #03-01
Singapore 048422 (Singapore)
T +65.62225780
studio@modonline.com
www.modonline.com

→ **192**

Moniteurs Communication Design

Ackerstraße 21–22
10115 Berlin (Germany)
T +49.30.2434560
F +49.30.24345656
info@moniteurs.de
www.moniteurs.de

→ **196**

Emmanuelle Moreaux architecture + design

T +81.3.32930323
F +81.3.32930322
contact@emmanuelle.jp

→ **166**

NOSIGNER

Mentlgasse 12a
6020 Innsbruck (Österreich)
T +43.512.586259
F +43.512.58625917
office@arch-hunger.at

→ **368**

Fabio Ongarato Design

1st Floor, 569 Church Street
Richmond, VIC 3121 (Australia)
T +61.3.94212344
F +61.3.94212655
press@ongarato.com.au
www.fabioongaratodesign.com.au

→ **78, 124, 140, 172**

P-06 Atelier

Rua Lino de Assunção, 48-50
2770-109 Paço de Arcos (Portugal)
T +351.213011834
F +351.213011835
atelier@p-06-atelier.pt
www.p-06-atelier.pt

→ **20**, **26**, **36**, **64**, **158**, **230**

Pentagram

204 Fifth Avenue
New York, NY 10010 (USA)
T +1.212.6837000
info@pentagram.com
www.pentagram.com
www.pentagram.com

→ **72**, **84**, **112**, **188**, **236**

PLAYFRAME

Kiefholzstraße 3
12435 Berlin (Germany)
T +49.30.200060420
F +49.30.200060429
info@playframe.de

→ **104**

R2 design

Rua de Meinedo, 112
4100-337 Porto (Portugal)
T +351.229386865
F +351.22.6174915
mail@r2design.pt
www.r2design.pt

→ **24**, **38**, **86**

Raffinerie AG für Gestaltung

Anwandstrasse 62
8004 Zürich
T +41.43.3221111
F +41.43.3221110
contact@raffinerie.com

→ **40**

Ralston & Bau

Transplant / 6963 Dale i Sunnfjord / Norway
T +47.57735597
F +47.48899213190
about@ralstonbau.com
www.ralstonbau.com

→ **190**

Rockwell Group

5 Union Square West, 8th Floor
New York, NY, 10003 (USA)
T +1. 212.4630334
F +1.212.4630335
newbusiness@rockwellgroup.com
www.rockwellgroup.com

→ **243**

Redmond Schwartz Mark Design

160 Avenida Cabrillo
San Clemente, CA 92672 (USA)
T +1.949.4929479
F +1.949.4922230
sanclemente@rsmdesign.net
www.rsmdesign.net

→ **146**

Teresa Sapey Estudio de Arquitectura

Calle Ruiz de Alarcón 7
28014 Madrid (Spain)
T +34.91.7450876
F +34.91.5644300
info@teresasapey.com
www.teresasapey.com

→ **224**, **234**, **242**

Nikolaus Schmidt Design

Schleifmühlgasse 7/11
1040 Vienna (Austria)
T +43.664.3458709
F +43.1.9680311
contact@nikolausschmidt.com
www.nikolausschmidt.com

→ **184**

SenseTeam

City of Garden Shucheng Road
Luohu District,Shenzhen, P.R.C.
PC 518029 (China)
T +86.755.82484277
F +86.755.82484645
sensebrand@hotmail.com
www.sensebrand.com/blog/

→ **22**

Sid Lee

75 Queen Street, Office 1400
Montrèal, QC
H3C 2N6 (Canada)
T +1.514.282.2200
info@sidlee.com
www.sidlee.com

→ **114**, **144**

Silk Pearce

57 Priory Street
Colchester, Essex C01 2QE (United Kingdom)
T +44.1206.871001
design@silkpearce.com
www.silkpearce.com

→ **44**

Adi Stern Design

Head of the Visual Communication Department Bezalel
Academy of Arts and Design, Jerusalem
T +972.2.5893323
adi@bezalel.ac.il

→ **12**

Studio FM Milano

Via Fioravanti 30
20154 Milan (Italy)
T +39.02.89656230
F +39.02.89656223
info@studiofmmilano.it
www.studiofmmilano.it

→ **46**

Erik Schmitt and Julio Martinez/ Studio1500

524 Washington Street
San Francisco, CA 94111 (USA)
T +1.415.951500
contact@studio1500sf.com
www.studio1500sf.com

→ **56, 62, 63**

Sweden Graphics

Bondegatan 11
11623 Stockholm (Sweden)
T + 46.708601291
nille@swedengraphics.com
www.swedengraphics.com

→ **48**

Naoki Terada/ Terada Design Architects

2-19-23 Bdg.2F Kabukicho Shinjuku-ku
Tokyo (Japan)
T +81.3.64135700
F +81.3.64135701
info@teradadesign.com
www.teradadesign.com

→ **80, 210**

TROIKA

Arch 355
Laburnum Street
London E2 8BB (United Kingdom)
T +44.20.77293255
studio@troika.uk.com
www.troika.uk.com

→**58**

Nicolas Vrignaud

47 Rue de la Villette
75019 Paris (France)
T +33.1.420810 04
atelier@b-headroom.com
www.b-headroom.com

→ **135**

Büro für Gestaltung Wangler & Abele

Büro für Gestaltung Wangler & Abele
Hohenzollernstraße 89
80796 Munich (Germany)
T +49.89.27370260
F +49.89.27370280
info@bfgest.de
www.bfgest.de

→ **88, 116, 119, 206, 212**

Zup Associati Design

Via Manfredo Fanti, 6 c/o
Perugia 06121 (Italy)
T +39.075.5738714
F +39.075.5725268
zup@zup.it
www.zup.it

→ **68, 244**

Satoshi Asakawa — 138-139
Courtesy of bauer konzept & gestaltung — 14-15, 162-163
Kris Baum + Stephen Minning — 220-223
Peter Bennetts — 18-19
Brett Boardman — 96-97
Courtesy of BOSCO — 16-17
Marcus Bredt — 116-117, 119
Courtesy of BWM Architekten und Partner — 61
CI&A Photography — 192
Peter Clarke — 78-79
Daniel Colombo — 142-143, 202-203
Courtesy of compactlab — 76-77, 100-101
Tinko Czetwertynski — 34-35
Courtesy of D&AD — 83, 90-91
Carsten de Riese — 206-207
Earl Carter Photography — 172-173
Courtesy of emerystudio — 160-161, 174-175, 228-229
Courtesy of P-06 Atelier, FG+SG
 architectural photography — 26-27, 36-37, 64-67
Courtesy of Frost* Design — 54-55, 126-129,
 148-149, 149, 215, 216-217
Courtesy of Gabor Palotai Design — 134
Nelson Garrido — 86-87
Ricardo Gonçalves — 20-21, 158-159
Brigida González — 28-29
Courtesy of Gourdin & Müller — 108-111, 136-137
Courtesy of Graphical House — 193
Giuseppe Greco — 230-233
Courtesy of großgestalten
 kommunikationsdesign — 204 r.
Courtesy of Gruppe Gut — 52-53
Courtesy of Günter Hermann Architekten — 60
Fernando Guerra — 38-39
Roland Halbe — 200-201
Florian Hammerich — 170-171, 182-183
Michael Heinrich — 164-165
Courtesy of Henkelhiedl — 102-103
Hans Jüregen Landes — 88-89
Bruno Klomfar — 184-187
Andreas Koerner — 98-99, 194-195, 200-201, 241
Luuk Kramer — 240
Courtesy of KW43 BRANDDESIGN — 180-181
Courtesy of Latitude Group — 218-219
Shannon McGrath — 124-125
Rudi Meisel — 212-213
Costantine Meyer — 178-179
Courtesy of Mike and Maaike Inc. — 214
Courtesy of Mind Design — 106-107, 118, 154-155

Studio Commercial, Stephen Minning — 196-197
Nacása & Partners Inc. — 122-123, 132-133, 176-177
Hidehiko Nagaishi — 166169
Yoki Omori — 80-81, 210-211
Pablo Orcajo — 224-227
Jamie Padgett — 63
Courtesy of Pentagram — 72-73, 84-85, 112-113,
 188-189, 236-239
Cesare Querci — 30-33
Courtesy of R2 design — 24-25
Courtesy of Raffinerie AG für Gestaltung — 40-43
Courtesy of Red Dot — 82, 130-131, 204-205
Christian Richters — 200-201
Courtesy of Rockwell Group — 243
Rossano Ronci — 33 a.,b.l
Courtesy of Red Dot, Liang Rong — 22
Courtesy of D&AD, Lukas Roth — 23
Courtesy of Redmond Schwartz Mark
 Design — 147
Tomohiro Sakashita — 94-95
Courtesy of Teresa Sapey Estudio
 de Arquitectura — 234-235, 242-243
Courtesy Adi Stern Design, Elad Sarig — 12-13
Erik Schmitt — 56-57, 62-63
Andrea Sestito — 208-209
Courtesy of Sid Lee — 114-115, 144-145
Courtesy of Silk Pearce — 44-45
João Silveira Ramos — 232-233
Courtesy of Studio FM Milano — 46-47
Katarina Stuebe — 59 b.r.
Courtesy of Sweden Graphics — 48-51
TROIKA — 58 l.
Bernd Vogel — 246-247
Courtesy of Nicolas Vrignaud — 135
Mark Whitfield — 150-153
David Zadig — 190 (portrait)
Courtesy of Zup Associati Design — 68-69

All other pictures, especially portraits and plans, were made available by the designers.

Front cover, from above to below, from left to right:
Pablo Orcajo, Earl Carter Photography, Courtesy of Sweden Graphics, Nacása & Partners Inc., Courtesy of bauer konzept & gestaltung, Nelson Garrido, Courtesy of Bosco Andreas Koerner, Courtesy of emerystudio
Back cover, from left to right:
Courtesy of R2 design, Courtesy of Latitude Group

IMPRINT

The Deutsche Bibliothek lists this publication in the
Deutsche Nationalbibliografie; detailed bibliographical
data are available on the internet at http://dnb.d-nb.de
//
ISBN 978-3-03768-091-9

© 2012 by Braun Publishing AG
www.braun-publishing.ch
//

1st edition 2012
//
Editor and layout: Michelle Galindo
Graphic concept: ON Grafik | Tom Wibberenz
Reproduction: Bild1Druck GmbH, Berlin
//